Praise for the adult edition of

The Far Away Brothers

★ "Powerful. . . . One of the most searing books on illegal immigration since Sonia Nazario's *Enrique's Journey*."
—*Kirkus Reviews*, Starred

"Impeccably timed, intimately reported and beautifully expressed."
—*The New York Times*

"You should read *The Far Away Brothers*. We all should."
—NPR

"Timely and thought-provoking."
—*Publishers Weekly*

"Affecting and personal."
—*Library Journal*

NAMED ONE OF THE BEST BOOKS OF THE YEAR BY THE *NEW YORK TIMES BOOK REVIEW*

WINNER OF THE RIDENHOUR BOOK PRIZE

A CALIFORNIA BOOK AWARD SILVER MEDAL WINNER

A *LOS ANGELES TIMES* BOOK PRIZE FINALIST

SHORTLISTED FOR THE J. ANTHONY LUKAS BOOK PRIZE

LONGLISTED FOR THE PEN/JACQUELINE BOGRAD WELD AWARD FOR BIOGRAPHY

THE
FAR AWAY
BROTHERS

TWO TEENAGE IMMIGRANTS
MAKING A LIFE IN AMERICA

LAUREN MARKHAM

ADAPTED FOR YOUNG ADULTS

DELACORTE PRESS

All rights reserved. Published in the United States by Delacorte Press, an imprint of Random House Children's Books, a division of Penguin Random House LLC, New York.

This work is based on *The Far Away Brothers*, copyright © 2017 by Lauren Markham. Originally published in hardcover in the United States by Crown, an imprint of the Crown Publishing Group, a division of Penguin Random House LLC, New York, in 2017, and subsequently published in paperback by Broadway Books, an imprint of the Crown Publishing Group, in 2018.

Delacorte Press is a registered trademark and the colophon is a trademark of Penguin Random House LLC.

Visit us on the Web! GetUnderlined.com

Educators and librarians, for a variety of teaching tools, visit us at
RHTeachersLibrarians.com

Library of Congress Cataloging-in-Publication Data
Names: Markham, Lauren, author. | Adaptation of (work): Markham, Lauren. Far away brothers.
Title: The far away brothers : two teenage immigrants making a life in America / Lauren Markham.
Description: First edition. | New York : Delacorte Press, 2018. | Adapted from a work of the same title published for adults in 2017 by Crown. | Summary: Identical twins Ernesto and Raul Flores, seventeen, must flee El Salvador, make a harrowing journey across the Rio Grande and the Texas desert, face capture by immigration authorities, and struggle to navigate life in America.
Identifiers: LCCN 2018025469 | ISBN 978-1-9848-2977-1 (hc) | ISBN 978-1-9848-2978-8 (glb) | ISBN 978-1-9848-2979-5 (el)
Subjects: LCSH: Flores, Ernesto, 1997– —Juvenile literature. | Flores, Raul, 1997– —Juvenile literature. | Salvadorans—California—Oakland—Biography—Juvenile literature. | Salvadoran Americans—California—Oakland—Biography—Juvenile literature. | Illegal aliens—United States—Biography—Juvenile literature. | Refugees—California—Oakland—Social conditions—Juvenile literature. | Unaccompanied immigrant children—United States—Juvenile literature. | Twin brothers—Biography—Juvenile literature. | United States—Emigration and immigration—Juvenile literature. | El Salvador—Emigration and immigration—Juvenile literature.
Classification: LCC E184.S15 M37 2018 | DDC 979.4/66004687284—dc23

The text of this book is set in 11-point Sabon.
Interior design by Trish Parcell

Printed in the United States of America
10 9 8 7 6 5 4 3 2 1
First Edition

Random House Children's Books
supports the First Amendment and celebrates the right to read.

For Ben

CONTENTS

AUTHOR'S NOTE

A few years before writing this book, I received an assignment to travel to South Texas and write about the recent uptick in immigrant children crossing the border and what happened to them once they'd made it into the United States. In particular, I was focusing on unaccompanied minors: children who cross alone into the United States without papers or their parents. These children ranged in age from infants to age seventeen. Today, as in 2012 when I was first given my assignment, most of these young people were coming from countries in Central America that had grown increasingly dangerous due to gang violence and political unrest. The article's purpose was to let readers know what happened to these kids once they got to the United States, so I spent that spring digging into the massive infrastructure of apprehending, detaining, caring for, and litigating the cases of thousands of young migrants. In that year, unaccompanied minors more than tripled their historical annual average.

In the process of reporting this story about unaccompanied minors, I ended up with even more questions than when I began. I started working on another story, and then another, in hopes of finding more answers to the big questions about these important social issues. But I couldn't stop asking questions, and each question led to yet another. Why were these kids coming to the United States, and why so many? What were these children really risking—and enduring—to come here, and what was the likelihood they would gain the right to stay? Would they really be better off if they did? Were their stories of the terrifying journey and the gang violence overblown, and could I take their reasons for coming to the United States at face value?

In addition to writing, I work at a high school for immigrant youth in Oakland, California—a school I helped launch over a decade ago. Generally, these two professional worlds and my responsibilities in them—one as a journalist, one as an educator—have felt completely separate. My work in Oakland keeps me deeply grounded in communities at home, while my reporting has taken me to places like Slovenia, Thailand, Brazil, Peru, El Salvador, Texas, Alaska, Mexico, Kenya, and Ethiopia. I never expected for my two careers to merge so thoroughly, for my work as a reporter to take me deeper into the world of the school where I spent nearly all my time. My reporting on unaccompanied minors changed everything.

Just after I had another big story going to press about unaccompanied minors, Mr. David, my coworker at Oakland International High School, came into my office. "We really need to do something about all the kids with upcoming court dates."

What?

It turned out that a number of our newest students had been ordered to appear in immigration court in the coming months. Like the kids I had been reporting about all over the country, these new students at Oakland International were unaccompanied minors, too. By that spring of 2014, more than sixty unaccompanied minors had enrolled at Oakland International High School out of a student body of just under four hundred. By the following fall, the number surpassed ninety. Today, in 2018, unaccompanied minors make up nearly a third of Oakland International High School's student population.

Imagine being seventeen, having traveled alone through treacherous terrain to reach a new country. You braved the desert, corrupt police and immigration officials, migrant profiteers. You heard stories of kidnappings, rapes, murders, of people losing life and limb underneath trains, of dying of thirst in the desert. And once you finally make it to the United States, you're arrested and put into detention, then ordered deported.

Pending your deportation hearing, you're released into the care of an adult, but you're in a new country where you don't speak the language. You need a lawyer, but you don't know where to find one and you don't have any money. The notion of court is terrifying, as is the prospect of being deported back home. You left home, after all, because your life was in danger—the gangs were after you, or a family member, or the violence had gotten so bad you could no longer safely go to school, or your family didn't have enough money to put food on the table. Now you're far from your loved ones and have few people, if any, caring for your basic needs in this new country. Before you arrived, the United States felt like the promised land, but now it feels like a massive, terrifying maze, or even, at times, a cage.

I heard dozens of stories like these from my students. They amazed me with their resilience; many also struggled deeply. After my conversation with Mr. David, I spent many afternoons shepherding kids to pro bono (free) legal agencies and court dates, and setting up intake appointments and "know your rights" information sessions at the school. The students needed counseling, tutoring, and doctors' appointments; some of them needed help finding homeless shelters and access to food and clothing. Supporting unaccompanied minors quickly became one of my primary responsibilities.

In February 2014, I met the Flores twins (To protect the anonymity of the "Flores" family, I have changed their names and those of many others who appear in this book, as well as the name of their hometown). Getting to know them deepened my perspective on the causes, challenges, and prospects of young immigrants coming to this country today. I could not stop thinking about their story.

In the summer of 2014, a few months after I met the twins and began working with them almost daily to help them find a lawyer, heal from their traumas, secure housing, and put down tenuous roots in Oakland, the media began reporting about unaccompanied minors. Day and night, stories of young migrants—kids like the Flores twins traveling alone from El Salvador, Guatemala, and Honduras—were all over the airwaves, the TV stations, the newspapers. The twins, as well as other students, told me that the stories they were hearing were incomplete; the media representations of young immigrants didn't seem fair. After all, how can you sum up a whole life, and the complexities of a person's choice to leave home—if it can even be considered much of a choice at all—in just a few columns of a newspaper, or a brief sound byte on TV?

Eventually, I asked the twins (and later, their family members back in El Salvador) if they would consider sharing their story with others. They agreed, and though there are other lives and perspectives included in these pages, their story is at the heart of this book.

To learn more about the Flores family's story, and the stories of the hundreds of thousands of migrants like them, I traveled to El Salvador, Mexico, Guatemala, and Texas, reporting from various fulcrums of violence in El Salvador as well as stations along the migrant trail north. Parts of this book were things I witnessed myself, and other parts have been reconstructed through extensive reporting and interviews—all in service of telling the larger story about the changing dynamics of migration across the United States' southern border.

Since reporting that first article years ago, I have heard countless stories from young people traveling alone to reach the United States. Every story is different, but they also bear remarkable similarities, often having to do with mounting violence in the children's home countries. These girls and boys are crossing into the United States in search of the fabled "better life" that has attracted migrants, authorized and unauthorized, since before the *Mayflower* landed. For many in the Northern Triangle—Honduras, Guatemala, and El Salvador—a "better life" means a life where they are not afraid of being killed simply because they are young and poor and born in the wrong place at the wrong time.

Those of us whose ancestors aren't native to this land, or whose ancestors weren't forcibly brought to this land, are descended from immigrants or are immigrants ourselves. Immigration has shaped this country and made it what it is today. Yet throughout history, when a new group of immigrants arrives, they are more often than not met with a new version of old persecution. It was once true that the Irish, Italians, and Greeks (my great-grandmother was from Greece) were scorned, ridiculed, and barred from employment, housing, and school. Chinese immigrants were excluded from this country by law; Japanese Americans were interned in concentration camps; Jewish refugees were kept out of the country in spite of the horrors of the Holocaust. The list goes on and on. Xenophobia—the fear and distrust of those perceived to be "other"—hasn't gone away, it just has found new targets.

But this book isn't just an immigration story; it's also a story about trying to find a place in a vast, complex, and often cruel world. The teenage twins at the heart of this book, as well as the dozens of other young people included in these pages, are all searching for belonging and acceptance. The process of growing up requires asking big questions, which often lack easy answers: Who am I, where do

I come from, who do I want to become, and where do I fit into an imperfect world? In the context of immigration, these questions are even harder. In a country where a shifting administration has changed the policy toward those seeking refuge, and now some of the most powerful politicians are sending the message that new immigrants are not welcome, how are young people like the Flores brothers supposed to feel about who they are and what it means to live in the United States of America today?

This book began as a series of questions. Answering these questions became my personal imperative, one that would help me better understand my students, my country, and the endless churn of southern migration into the United States. The story of the Flores twins isn't the most harrowing, or the most unjust, or the most extraordinary I've come across as an educator and a journalist. But something in their story roundly and heartbreakingly illustrates the wounds of war, the spirit of a new generation of immigrants, and the impact of migration on the United States—as well as on the country of El Salvador.

Whether your family has lived here for a long time or you have just arrived, you are probably trying to find your place in the world. This work focuses on the young Central Americans coming here in unprecedented numbers to accomplish the same thing. How they are or are not received and supported will determine, in part, the next chapter in the American story. This is a book about who these young men and women are, where they come from, and the choices they've made. It is about what their stories reveal about who we are as a country, and what we will, or might, become.

THE
FAR AWAY
BROTHERS

PROLOGUE

It's a few minutes after nine o'clock, and the Flores twins are buckled into the back seat of Wilber's Toyota, lurching through downtown San Francisco in search of the courthouse. As their older brother brakes and curses his way through the morning traffic, Raúl's and Ernesto's identical faces press against the windows as they hunt for street names and building numbers. They are lost.

Their packet of immigration papers states the courthouse address (100 Montgomery Street) and the date and time they've been ordered to appear: February 19, 2014, at ten a.m. This morning they left the apartment with a two-hour window. It's important to be not just on time, but *early*, in the Estados Unidos, Wilber said.

Wilber groans as they stop in the middle of a crowded intersection. At twenty-four, he is now, for lack of a better option, his brothers' guardian. He'd signed a paper promising to provide for their basic needs, to feed and clothe them, to enroll them in school, and to get them to court on time. In his seven years here, he'd become somewhat of an expert on the United States and its rules. A rule of the landscaping business, for instance: no work, no pay. He'd miss another day of wages today to get his brothers to court.

The twins have been dreading this appointment for months, ever since they were picked up out of the Texas desert, their shoes ripped to raggedy shreds, their bodies dizzy with thirst. They thought for sure they'd be deported right away, back to El Salvador and all that awaited them there.

But they weren't. They were taken to a detention center, where a woman explained to them that, since they were under eighteen, they'd have a choice: they could opt to go back to El Salvador on their own—*impossible*—or they could go to court and fight for the right to stay.

Court? In front of a judge? They'd need a lawyer, for starters, and the prospect of obtaining official papers seemed absurd. Why, out of all the undocumented people like them, should they—kids who'd been here only a few months—get papers?

It is 9:06. They have just under an hour. Wilber has plugged the address into his phone's GPS, but it seems to have stopped working altogether.

At seventeen, the twins have never been to a city before— unless you count the outskirts of San Salvador, which they'd been to only a few times to visit relatives, or Mexico City, where they passed through with their *coyota*, the woman

2

who guided them across the border. San Francisco looms like no other place they've ever seen. Raúl used to picture these buildings in the quiet nights back home, rising upward like ladders, like possibilities. But now that he's under them, they just make him feel, as most things in the United States of America so far do, small and out of place.

The twins still have the lingering feeling of being chased, of needing to look over their shoulders. Every few nights now, Ernesto wakes up screaming, drenched in sweat. He won't talk about it, but Raúl knows his brother. He knows how afraid Ernesto was before he was run out of town. And during that night in the desert weeks later. The road can change a person.

The shelter staff members had explained how court works: the judge will come in, and everyone will stand. The judge will say their names, and they should respond *presente*, here. Last night the boys reviewed what they remembered. Look the judge in the eyes, they reminded each other. In the United States, their instructors told them, looking down makes you appear disrespectful.

When they get to court, what will they even say to the judge? With no lawyer, no English, no idea what to argue on their own behalf, they worry they'll be deported this very day. And then what?

Nine-thirty, nine-thirty-five. Another confused, traffic-laden circuit loops them back to Market Street.

Wilber cranks the heat high. Outside it's cold, and the twins haven't brought anything to wear over their almost-matching blue plaid shirts, their nicest items of clothing. Wilber bought them, like practically everything they have.

3

Both boys have tucked the shirts into their skinny jeans, hiked up higher than usual with the help of belts, and they've laced their sneakers tightly, instead of leaving them loose-tied like the kids at school. Ernesto scoffed when he saw Raúl. "Copying me," he said. He removes his earrings—the characteristic the teachers at school use to tell them apart.

As ten o'clock approaches, Ernesto blinks rapidly, and Raúl breathes heavily through his nose, lips pressed into a tight, thin line.

"Should we ask somebody?" Raúl finally whispers.

Ernesto shoots him a look. *Who? Who would we possibly ask?* The twins barely speak English, and though Wilber can hold his own, how could he pull over a car in the middle of the downtown rush? In spite of his seven years here, Wilber feels just as much as his brothers do: that *immigrant* and *illegal* are painted onto him like a sign.

Ernesto wants to scream at his brother, *How long have you lived here? Can't you find us this fucking courthouse?* But his throat seems to have closed up. They'll miss their appointment, they'll be sent home, they'll wind up dead, and what would have been the point of any of it—the journey, the debt?

At a certain point, you just give up. The boys know it at the exact same moment, as with many things. Wilber feels it too. It's an hour past their appointment. It's over.

"Okay," Wilber says. The twins say nothing, just watch out the windows as the throng of people drifts away and the car turns onto the bridge. They won't go to school today, probably not tomorrow. It would be too easy for Immigration to find them. And *la migra*—the immigration authority—has Wilber's address, too. They could go hide out somewhere, but Wilber is the only person here they really know.

They've been hunted by gangs, by packs of wild coyotes in the desert, by bad spirits, by rumors, by debt, by *la migra*. They've been chewed up and spit out all over this godforsaken continent, and after all this, just for missing an appointment, they're sure they'll be delivered back to El Salvador for good. But they can't go back. For too long, the Flores twins have been running. They may have reached a dead end.

CHAPTER 1

"You boys from eighteen?" one of the young men asked, pointing his gun toward a graffiti tag on the wall: BARRIO 18.

It was 2008. The Flores twins, twelve, were playing cards on the town soccer field with their brother and friends when a pickup pulled up. Ten or so guys sporting baggy clothes and tattoos stood in the truck bed with guns and machetes. They were MS-13, or Mara Salvatrucha, the twins knew—members of the notorious gang. The MS-13 was showing up more and more in La Colonia, the small town where the Flores boys lived. The twins and their friends were high on adrenaline from having won a soccer match that morning. But the sight of the armed men scared them silent.

They shook their heads.

Ernesto's gaze was lowered, but he could feel the men staring down at him.

"I asked if you fuckers were from eighteen!" the man

shouted. At that, one of the twins' friends took off running into the woods. Suddenly Ernesto and Raúl were sprinting through the forest that flanked the town soccer field—Ernesto first, Raúl close behind—panting and crashing through the tall grasses while shouts and a scatter of gunshots crackled behind them.

Running away from a truck full of MS-13 gangsters was a risky choice. It either showed the kids' allegiance to the rival Barrio 18 gang or, at the very least, a lack of respect for MS-13.

When the shouts sounded far enough away, the twins hit the ground, lying on their bellies in the brush. They stayed there for what felt like hours—until they were sure the truck was gone.

The road to La Colonia weaves through a tangle of greenery: there are vines overhead, and tall, tight rows of banana trees, canopies of *barillos,* pink flowering cacao, and flourishing palms. La Colonia—which is about thirty miles from San Salvador and home to fewer than four thousand people—spreads up and around the slopes of a gentle, low hill.

The houses along the road are simple but comfortable, built from concrete, many of them painted colors that were once bright—ice blue, cotton-candy pink. Less fortunate homes dot the nearby hills and farmland. Flags of the ARENA conservative party flap from poles. Along the road stand La Colonia's schools—two high schools and an elementary school. One of only about a dozen Flores family photos is of the twins and their older sister, somber-faced and gangly beneath too-big dress clothes, on the proud occasion of Ernesto and Raúl's ninth-grade graduation.

Cows use the road as often as people do, plodding along between farm and pasture. During harvest time, families lay their bean pods and corn out to dry on the pavement, the kernels spread out like a mosaic.

The road crests the hill and then dips downward, and that's where the Flores home sits, a stone house lined with crumbling stucco. From there it's not much farther to the center of town, a sleepy square rimmed by a block or two of houses and a few businesses—family-run restaurants, shops, the mayor's office. The high-rising church is the town's main attraction.

Until the twins were teenagers, the town center was busy day and night. Kids ran around the playground or played soccer. Those who'd begged spare change from their parents bought snow cones from the woman with the stand. The *pupuserías* were open until midnight, playing music and serving sodas and beers, the proprietors flipping the cakes of corn *masa* against the griddle until the edges were crispy.

"It was a beautiful town," Raúl remembers. "It was."

Like the rest of the farmers in La Colonia, the twins' father, Wilber Sr., regarded the mountain and its fertile land as a divine inheritance. The land was good to him; God provided. "The way to survive this world is to stay close to God," he said to his children. "And keep *manos limpias*": clean hands.

Wilber carried a small Bible in his pocket at all times, the binding frayed and worn from use. He and his wife, Esperanza, had always wanted a big family, but for many years they'd felt they might be cursed. They got married in the midst of the country's civil war (1980–1992), in 1985. Two years later, as the war still raged, Esperanza gave birth to their first baby, Ricardo.

It was a dirty war, as Wilber put it. On one side there was the right-wing government, loyal to those with money, and operating with brutal military force. On the other there was the growing leftist guerrilla movement, claiming to be fighting for the interests of the poor, especially the country's rural farmers. But the Flores family thought it best to stay out of politics.

In cities and in the countryside, mutilated bodies showed up in the streets. Political prisoners were heaved off a cliff above San Salvador. Later, a 1993 report by the UN Truth Commission for El Salvador asserted that 85 percent of the atrocities were carried out by the conservative ARENA government. In fact, the United States helped to train and back these forces—death squads and all—to prevent a guerrilla takeover: an effort, in the midst of 1980s Cold War paranoia, to prevent the "spread" of Communism.

Soldiers marched through La Colonia on occasion. "The soldiers came looking for people," Esperanza explained. "They could mistake you for someone else and punish you for something they did." Sometimes Esperanza and the baby hid when Wilber was out working.

In 1990, as country-wide violence churned, Esperanza gave birth to another son: Wilber Jr. Then as peace negotiations were under way in Mexico City, she gave birth to a daughter who died at just several weeks old. Esperanza prayed for more children. The peace accords were signed in Mexico City in 1992, and as the government and the guerrillas agreed to lay down their weapons for good, Esperanza got pregnant again two more times. Each baby died. Was she indeed cursed?

In 1994, El Salvador held its first free and fair peacetime elections. The conservative ARENA party won, but the war was over. After so many years of conflict, it was a time of rebuilding. That year Esperanza's prayers were answered: she gave birth to her sixth child—a girl, Maricela. Maricela lived.

The Flores family were still farmers who scraped by, harvest to harvest; who struggled to find money to buy clothes or take a child to the doctor. But as Esperanza looked back, she regarded those as good years: three healthy babies alive, a country out of war.

At the end of 1995, when her belly began to swell, she prayed she wouldn't lose this one, too.

Within just three months she was bigger than she'd ever been at that stage. By month five she was exhausted. She began to have her own quiet suspicions. She didn't want to jinx it, but she thought she might be carrying two. She had a warm, warbling sense of it in her heart.

They saved up some money. When it neared her time to give birth, she took the bus down to the hospital, where they listened to her stomach and brought a picture onto the screen.

"Twins," the nurse said.

She'd been right. Fifteen days later she went into labor. Ernesto first, then Raúl twelve minutes later. Two identical babies. The nurses brought them both into her arms. They'd make it, she thought.

From the minute they were born, Ernesto and Raúl were inseparable. They had distinct personalities, but they resisted being apart. They wanted to sit next to each other in school, to eat together, to walk side by side to school, to work with their father in the fields in the same shifts.

When Ernesto and Raúl began to toddle down the road holding their mother's hands, neighbors and the occasional stranger would fall into prayer upon seeing them: two identical people. A miracle.

Teachers and family friends had a hard time distinguishing them. The siblings knew which was which, most of the time—Ernesto had a tiny mole under his eye. But since they were most often together, it was easier to refer to them as one: *los gemelos*, the twins.

When the twins were ten, their mother developed a cough and began cooking outside in the back courtyard. The twins took over the sooty former kitchen as their bedroom. They were delighted. Finally a space of their own.

A few years earlier Wilber had put the brothers to work

in the *milpa,* the crops out in the fields. There was Wilber's own land—two separate plots where they grew the corn and beans and tomatoes—and then the land they leased from the twins' godfather, who allowed them to plant and keep half the yield. Wilber Sr. needed all the workers he could get. For one thing he and Esperanza had more mouths to feed: since the twins, they had had Lucia, then Marina, then Pablo, then Luis. A family of eleven was large even for La Colonia. Wilber also wanted his kids to understand how to make a living off the land. Work would keep them out of trouble.

The twins got up with the sun and spent the mornings in the fields, then went to school for the afternoon session. This was the norm; because of overcrowding in schools (which was really due to underfunding by the conservative government), Salvadoran children attended school for only half a day, in either the morning or the afternoon. After school the twins' job was to take care of the livestock. Their days were long and without rest.

While Raúl was all playfulness, Ernesto could be hot-tempered. Ernesto was also more socially attuned: he studied the older, popular boys to be like them. Raúl made friends easily enough but wasn't all that worried about being included. He was the artsy one, often preferring drawing or painting to *futból,* or soccer. As they rooted into their own personalities, the contours of their faces seemed to change ever so slightly: Raúl's now appeared softer, more wide-eyed, whereas Ernesto was furrow-browed with a cultivated toughness.

"I'm the angel, and you're the devil," Raúl joked.

"But I'm the older one, so I have to be more serious and in charge," Ernesto retorted. They argued over who was taller, using their hair to claim additional height.

By fourth grade the twins ran with a steady pack of six boys from school. The group liked to pick on one another, play pranks, and call one another names, but the twins felt the others picked on them more often, and cut deeper.

"You're too poor for shoes. Look at those shoes—they're falling apart."

"Dark-ass peasant boys."

It was unfair, the twins thought, because many of these guys were even poorer than they were.

"Just stay away from them," their classmate Edgar warned. A kind, quiet boy, he was a more reliable friend than the others. Still, Ernesto, in particular, was drawn to that group.

"Your father's a beggar with that guitar of his," one bully, Silvio, declared. Wilber played guitar in church and sometimes sang hymns on the street. The other kids cackled. No one came to the twins' defense.

The teachers did little to protect them, and in fact, sometimes joined in at poking fun at them or their father. When a notebook appeared in the classroom scrawled with obscenities, which Ernesto knew to be Silvio's handiwork—he'd seen him do it—the teacher pointed the finger at Ernesto.

"Why did you do this?" he demanded.

"It wasn't me!" Ernesto insisted.

"Then who was it?"

But Ernesto wouldn't dare say. The teacher sent him home.

Raúl wasn't in trouble, but he followed his brother back up the hill without a second thought.

"They're always blaming us," Ernesto complained on the way home.

Raúl nodded.

Another day a kid hit Ernesto in the temple with a rock. A boy had thrown it on purpose. It bled and left a bruise for days; he'd have the scar there forever. When Esperanza asked what happened, Ernesto lied—he'd fallen playing soccer, he said.

Their own relatives fueled the bullying, too. Wilber's half sister, Graciela, had long looked down on Wilber. Things got worse when she'd married Don Agustín, a man from another town. Agustín was one of the town's big men, a guy with more land and cash than most. He and Graciela had a spacious house, a slick truck, and a profitable coffee crop. To them, Wilber's big family was a laughingstock and an embarrassment. As the twins grew up, the Floreses were invited to fewer weddings and family parties, then none.

In 2010, Uncle Agustín's house was robbed—people knew he had money. So he arranged for a private security force: Agustín would now be protected by gangs.

The gangs. The Floreses heard about the violence on the news first. It was spreading through El Salvador like a contagion. Bodies found dumped in secret grave sites, police officers murdered, women raped and killed. The whole world around them began to tremble.

The country's morgues began to fill up. If no one identified the corpses—or if the deceased didn't have a family, or the circumstances of the murder were such that it was best for the family to lie low—the body would be incinerated. Sometimes local police couldn't find a person thought to be killed. Too often, that person would become one of San Salvador's missing.

Most homicides are known to be the work of the gangs. Yet around 95 percent of crimes in the Northern Triangle go uncharged. To report a gang member for murder carries a near-certain death sentence for the accuser and often for his or her family, too. So people keep quiet; the bodies pile up.

The gangs were growing their armies by recruiting kids—particularly in San Salvador, but in smaller cities, too. The first of the infamous gangs had formed in the United States in the 1980s among Salvadoran exiles. They were made up of mostly undocumented youth, kids who had fled trauma, violence, and forced army recruitment during the Salvadoran civil war.

Like the Italian Mafia that rose to power in the early twentieth century, the Salvadoran gangs in Los Angeles were composed of young, impoverished immigrants from a society that was racist and prejudiced against them to begin with. Initially they formed gangs to protect themselves against other local gangs. Isolated, without money or a supportive community, many kids had nowhere to turn, and so formed allegiances with one another. These thousands of young men in Los Angeles were then incarcerated and deported back to El Salvador. Along with them came the gang culture.

In El Salvador, the gangs made their money off low-level drug deals or extortion, charging people a biweekly fee called *renta,* or rent. Most of the members were young, poor guys not unlike the twins. Some kids chose to join, while others fell into it unwittingly, asked to do favors here and there until they were in too deep to retreat. Joining could be a seduction—impoverished, parentless, or abused children were lured into a place of belonging with an opportunity to become someone whom others respected and feared.

Gang life did bring a feeling of power, but at great cost. Many of the gang leaders ran things from prison, and though the guys working the streets acquired the appearance of success—nicer clothes, a phone—they stayed poor.

When the twins were ten, a cousin of theirs was shot. He'd gotten on the wrong side of the gangs. The following year the body of an estranged uncle of theirs was found in the river a few miles away. He'd been murdered.

Signs of gang activity started to show up in town, too. One day they noticed MS-13 graffiti on a signpost near their house. They walked home more quickly then, heads down.

Kids began talking about *la violencia* and *la delincuencia* in school. "You know if it's a gangster because they dress good," one of their classmates said one day.

"If you're in a gang, you get rich," another explained. It didn't matter that it wasn't true.

Classmates started to throw gang signs. Hard to know,

at first, whether they were just posing, but you didn't mess with a kid who pledged any kind of allegiance. The twins watched who changed their style—who had the slick clothes, the swagger, the new phone.

The half day of school suited agricultural families like the Floreses, but it left many other children unoccupied, out in the streets, vulnerable. As the twins grew up, more youths were recruited by sheer force. A kid was often told that if he didn't join, the gangs would kill him or his mother, or rape his sister. The threat of violence seemed to hover everywhere.

The twins' parents didn't say much about the gangs, preferring, as always, to keep their distance. Their father reminded them, as they shoveled and pulled vegetables from the ground, that work would keep their hands clean.

CHAPTER 2

Out in the morning sun, Wilber Jr.—the second Flores son—plotted his escape from La Colonia. He loved his parents, but he felt they had been irresponsible. Really, nine children? The household's resources were stretched thin. Food was scarce. Meanwhile, the country was becoming more dangerous, it seemed, every day.

One spring day during his final year of high school, Wilber took the bus to a neighboring town to take the entrance exam for university. This was his escape plan. When he passed he figured he could raise enough money working some nearby coffee harvests to pay for school.

Right before he enrolled in a nearby college, his dad called him into his bedroom. It was evening, and Esperanza was outside cooking dinner.

"Son," he said, "do you want to go to the North?"

Like all Salvadorans who'd grown up after the massive

19

exodus—over 350,000 people—of the civil war years of 1980–1992, Wilber held a reverence for El Norte. "The North" was an often starry-eyed euphemism for the United States, where work and money and opportunity, despite messages sent home to the contrary, were thought to be plentiful.

Wilber Sr. could support only so many kids. His eldest son, Ricardo, had developed a drinking problem, and he didn't trust him to send money back. Wilber Jr., on the other hand, was smart and responsible. His father must have recognized, Wilber thought, that his namesake was a hard worker with big dreams outside La Colonia.

Of course Wilber Jr. wanted to go. He wanted to help support his family, but more than anything, he wanted to go to school in the United States. His plan was to learn English, enroll in college, make extra money to send back home, and earn his degree. It would be hard at first, sure, but in time he knew he could work his way up that ladder of the American Dream.

His father hired a *coyote,* a guide who would smuggle Wilber Jr. through the dangerous route north into the United States. To pay the *coyote,* he borrowed six thousand dollars from a lender. Wilber Jr. understood that he alone was responsible for the debt, and he would have to pay it off swiftly so the interest didn't swallow the family. But within a couple of weeks he'd be in the United States, he figured, and after a couple more, he'd have a job and be sending money home—probably hundreds of dollars each month. In 2007, when the twins were eleven years old and Wilber Jr. was seventeen, he left for the North. Wilber Sr.

slipped a small photograph of his son—a school portrait in black and white—into his fraying pocket Bible.

Wilber Jr. made it across on his first try. He called with the news that he'd reached San Jose, where they had a friend with whom he could stay, who had promised to help him find a job.

Wilber had become an *hermano lejano,* a faraway brother—a Salvadoran who had left the country and—most often—crossed into the United States. Along the road to the International Airport on the outskirts of San Salvador stands a large arc of stone with a sign reading WELCOME, FARAWAY BROTHER!

But they often don't return. El Salvador is home to 6.3 million people; nearly 2 million Salvadorans resided in the United States in 2013—a third of their home country's own population.

To Ernesto, it felt like he had lost his big brother–guardian. His sadness at this loss was laced with resentment: Wilber had this whole adventure ahead of him and was leaving his brothers behind to take over his share of the work. They'd probably never see him again.

Now that Wilber Jr. was gone, the twins had to guard the farm at night, sometimes sleeping in the barn and sometimes on the hillside under the stars. It was scary out there, the two of them alone, listening for rustles that could be crop thieves, or the armadillos that ruined the tomato plants, or bad spirits.

The idea of robbers didn't scare them so much—they

weren't really dangerous; just other poor people looking to swipe something to eat. What really scared them were the ghosts. Once, when they had lit a candle in a little shack near the barn, a long shadow emerged from nowhere. The shadow grew longer—until all of a sudden the candle blew out. The boys ran out of the shack screaming.

When dawn broke, the boys would stretch, dust themselves off, roll up their blankets, and head back to their home for breakfast. After a few more hours of sleep, they'd pull on their uniforms and go to school.

When the twins were in seventh grade, a new kid, Miguel, moved to town. He was a couple of years older than them. People whispered that his dad was a gangster, but then again, people also said Ernesto and Raúl's dad was a beggar. Ernesto started hanging out with Miguel at the soccer fields after school. He didn't seem like a gangster. He sometimes asked Ernesto and Raúl if he could take some of the tomatoes and corn from the fields home to his family. They always said yes. Within a few months they became friends with his crew from the high school. These older guys didn't pick on them at first, which was a relief.

The twins started working the coffee harvests in the nearby plantations, picking the beans until their fingers ached but earning extra cash to buy school supplies, clothes, and eventually a small, pay-as-you-go cell phone so they could use Facebook. One harvest, their older cousins Juan and Javier invited them to work on Uncle Agustín's coffee plantation. But when payday came, Agustín stiffed them, paying them only a fraction of what they should have received. He just looked at them and handed over a few dollars for many days of work, as if daring them to challenge him. They wouldn't, and he knew it.

"He thinks he can do whatever he wants because he's with the gangsters," Raúl murmured as they walked home, famished and exhausted.

"He can," Ernesto spat.

They had stopped asking their father why his side of the family hated them so much. Whatever the truth of the story, Wilber simply said Agustín was jealous of their work ethic. To Ernesto and Raúl, however, it was clear enough that their relatives were ashamed of them.

Juan and Javier passed along the notion of the twins' inferiority to other people in town. Soon enough, Miguel taunted them, too. But the tormenting would pass, and they would all still play soccer again, or walk home from school together, or go down to the river for a swim, or, as the years went on, for a smoke. Ernesto in particular clung to the prospect of joining Miguel's inner circle.

Eventually Miguel admitted to Ernesto that his father was in a gang. He told him that his dad had tattoos marking his allegiance to MS-13 and kept guns in the house. They lived poor, though. Even after all the tomatoes and beans the Floreses had given to Miguel, the twins once saw Miguel's dad robbing their corn crop. They never said anything, mostly out of fear, but also out of shame on behalf of Miguel's family. It was upsetting to be stolen from but even more humiliating to have to steal in order to eat. Is that what gang life amounted to—stealing corn?

• • •

The boys sprouted into adolescence, growing taller and ganglier. A year or so after the truck incident, they went to the river for a swim to cool off before getting to work in the fields. When they came through the brush onto the main road, a pack of young men—well-dressed with darting eyes—started following them.

They recognized one of the guys as their rumored half brother, Wilber's supposed son with a woman before Esperanza. Wilber denied the boy was his, but who knew. Either way this guy had always seemed to hate the Flores family. The twins had heard that he had fallen in with Juan and Javier and the local MS-13 ring. When the twins saw him leading the pack, they quickened their pace.

By now, gangs were no longer confined to just those communities of deportees sent back from Los Angeles in the 1990s. They were a large-scale network of criminals, with allies all across the world.

La Colonia was a full-fledged MS-13 territory. Around the region—sometimes in the twins' own town—people were shot and left in the bushes, their corpses half rotten by the time they were found. Heads were cut off, the dead left out in the centers of towns for all to see. Bodies turned up sprayed with bullets. When they heard the brutal reports, Wilber would sigh. Devil's work. "We're at war again," he said, shaking his head. A war between the government and the gangs, and between the gangs and each other.

The twins turned back to look, hoping their followers would be gone, but there they were, stone-faced, gaining on them. Finally Ernesto and Raúl approached a friend's house and ducked inside to call the police. The twins could see the pack outside the windows, waiting. Calling the police might only invite payback later, but how else would they get home? The police never came. Eventually the guys across the street left. The twins sprinted home and stayed indoors that night, asking Ricardo to take their shift up on the hill.

That crew never bothered Ernesto and Raúl again, though the twins saw them around town. Afterward the twins spent less time outside and more time at home, playing ball in the back courtyard. The town square grew quieter as people moved around La Colonia with more care. Practically no one was out at night anymore; one wouldn't dare.

Wilber Jr. called from time to time, though the twins rarely talked to him. He had gotten a landscaping job and sent monthly payments until his six-thousand-dollar *coyote* debt was gone. Then they heard from him less and less. He sent some money now and then—fifty, one hundred, two hundred dollars. The little bursts of cash allowed them to buy rice and milk and sugar to supplement their dwindling harvest. But then the money would be finished, and they wouldn't hear from Wilber for months.

"He only helped himself," their sister Maricela said. The twins had to agree.

Esperanza was more generous; she didn't fault her son. "The dream is always more difficult when you're awake," she said.

The dream could easily lure a person in. Edgar—their

quiet, steadfast friend from school—had never mentioned leaving. And yet one day, as the twins scurried to his door, his mother stopped them.

"Edgar's not here. He went to the North," she said, and shut the door.

CHAPTER 3

Being twins already made Raúl and Ernesto stand out. Dressing the same made it worse. When they turned thirteen, they decided to create their own, distinct styles.

They also decided that they needed a bicycle. A bike would give them bragging rights and, better yet, freedom. They imagined reaching the peak just beyond their house, mounting the bike together, and flying hands-free into town, kings of the road.

They couldn't afford to buy a bike, so they and their cousin made a deal with the local repair shop: they would get a bicycle in exchange for a sack and a half of corn— almost seventy-five pounds. One afternoon, when no one else was home, the twins loaded a sack onto their shoulders, then trudged into town. Their cousin met them there, with a stolen sack of his own. The owner handed over the bike.

It was red and sleek, shimmering with newness. The boys

fought over who could ride it on his own, who would pedal standing up as the other two balanced above the wheels, one on the handlebars and the other on the seat. They had to keep the bike a secret from their parents, but they also wanted to show it off to their friends.

For an entire week they hid the bike in the bushes by their house, hopping on each evening to ride it to the barn. But Wilber Sr. soon discovered it.

He took the twins into their bedroom. "Stealing from your own family?" he shouted. That bike cost food that they needed. It wasn't infrequent for Wilber Sr. to punish them with a rope, and that night was no exception.

They regretted the lying and stealing, and they still had scars as souvenirs. But they cherished the memory of the bike, the thrill of careening into the distance, the feeling of freedom.

People left La Colonia all the time—adults, kids, sometimes whole families. After their friend Edgar left, the twins day-dreamed about it more often. They imagined the places where people they knew had ended up—Arizona, Texas, California. Ernesto idealized El Norte just as his older brother had: a place with jobs, more stuff, opportunity. In El Norte, maybe he could have a bike in a matter of weeks. Wilber wrote home every now and again about how hard it was to make money, but Ernesto never quite believed it. He imagined his brother with nice clothes, a car, Nikes.

Raúl dreamed of the North, too, but differently. He con-jured it in his mind, especially the skyscrapers with gleaming windows. He was interested in seeing it but not in living there. He didn't want to be a farmer like his father, but he took Wilber Jr. at his word about life being harder up there than they'd been led to believe. Raúl had chosen his career track: banking. He was getting grades high enough to consider it. The good life he imagined for himself was in El Salvador.

Ernesto wasn't so sure.

"Want to get drunk?" one of their friends asked one day when they were fourteen. They'd never been drunk before, but Ernesto was in, and Raúl by extension was too. They pooled cash with their friends and bought a bottle at the cantina, which sold to kids as long as they had the money. They didn't know what kind of alcohol it was—just that it was clear and nearly made them vomit. At the banks of the river, Ernesto grabbed the bottle for a second round and slugged it back theatrically, to the cheers of the other boys.

Raúl, the quiet, timid giggler, was still the same old teasable Flores boy. But Ernesto had warrior potential.

A couple of older kids approached sixteen-year-old Ernesto in the hall one day, away from the other students.

"Silvio is always picking on you," one said. He nodded.

"Your friends too," another said.

"They won't mess with you if you come with us." They showed him their shoes, new and nice, and flashed their phones. "You should join," they told him, meaning MS-13.

Ernesto shook his head. "Nah," he said.

"You really should," the first guy replied.

He said he'd think about it and went back to class. He didn't tell Raúl.

The gangs were everywhere. Going outside was dangerous. Crowded markets became sites for running goods—money or drugs—back and forth, for collecting rent, for recruitment, for generally keeping an eye on things. One morning in the small town where Esperanza sometimes sold tomatoes, more than forty men were arrested for murders in the area.

Meanwhile, the boys who'd tried to recruit Ernesto claimed the sidewalks in the town center. Just a little stealing here, they had explained to Ernesto, a little rent collecting there. No big thing.

A friend invited Ernesto to a funeral in the next town over. The deceased, someone Ernesto had met only a couple of times, had been twenty years old. Inside the house the family members and friends wailed around the open casket. Ernesto said a prayer and felt queasy. The boy's face was bloated and unnatural-looking. A bullet had punctured his skull.

"Did you think about what we talked about?" the boys asked Ernesto at school.

"Yeah," he said. "But I can't."

"You sure?"

He couldn't tell if it was a threat or not. "I'm sure."

He told Raúl on the way home from school. "I won't join," he said. "I would never."

But Raúl wasn't totally convinced.

After that, Ernesto started to spend more time in town

after school, more time away from the family and his twin. "Just hanging out," he told Raúl. "Just playing soccer."

We measure water in gallons or liters, distance in miles or kilometers, height in feet or meters. Murders are measured in units of one hundred thousand. In 2011, when the twins were fifteen—prime gang-recruiting age—the murder rate was at an all-time high: seventy-one out of one hundred thousand people. That meant 4,354 murders out of a population of six million people, amounting to an average of twelve people murdered a day. By comparison, in 2015, the *Washington Post* reported that the United States, a country that is fifty times the size of El Salvador, had only four times the number of homicides.

People wanted—they *needed*—to get out to stay alive.

Between 1980 and 1990, the most brutal years of the civil war, approximately 371,000 Salvadorans migrated to the United States, out of a population of around five million—7 percent of the country's overall population. Looking for both refuge and economic opportunity, they moved north in a steady stream.

After the war, Salvadorans kept leaving—for economic opportunity, to reunite with family, and because an earthquake and several hurricanes destroyed livelihoods and sent people packing. By 2008, 1.1 million foreign-born Salvadorans lived in the United States.

It was during the fall of 2011, amid a stark increase of gang violence, that the number of kids leaving El Salvador for the United States skyrocketed. Friends, neighbors, and family members were leaving or were gone. The US media called the solo, underage crossers "unaccompanied minors"—kids traveling without papers or parents. By the end of fiscal year 2012, the number of unaccompanied minors nabbed by *la migra* and turned over to the Office of Refugee Resettlement (ORR) had nearly doubled since the year before, reaching 13,625. Twenty-seven percent of 2012's unaccompanied minors was from El Salvador.

Meanwhile, the number of undocumented adults started going down in almost inverse proportion to the rise in un-accompanied minors: from 1.1 million adult apprehensions in 2005 to 326,034 in 2012. With the tanking of the US economy, why go north to beg for jobs that aren't there? It was the children now, not so much the adults, who were moving north.

Unlike most people in the town, who dressed in worn farm-ing clothes, Uncle Agustín always had on a collared shirt and sunglasses. Agustín had figured out how to make the gang wars work for him.

He began to lend cash at high interest rates, which gave him enough money for a bigger enterprise: a *coyote* ring that, for a fee, helped people navigate the dangerous routes north. Agustín had some guys who would smuggle people through Guatemala and into Mexico, and get them across to the United States. The price was steep—seven thousand dollars or so—and it would increase over time as the in-terest piled up. When migrants couldn't pay the full fee,

Agustín was said to lend them money at 10 to 20 percent interest. Then he'd take their properties as collateral, as backup, if they didn't manage to pay.

The richer Agustín grew, the more often he hired gangs as a security force. Agustín's proximity to the gangs meant that Juan and Javier, and by extension many of the boys in the twins' circle, were spending more time around MS-13.

In 2012, the Salvadoran government, then led by the leftist Farabundo Martí National Liberation Front (FMLN) party, made a controversial decision: it would negotiate a truce with key gang leaders. So, government representatives, faith leaders, and the leaders of the powerful MS-13 and Barrio 18 gangs met at one of the country's highest-security prisons to make a deal. The gangs agreed to a cease-fire, allegedly in exchange for lighter prison sentences and more privileges for the gang leaders in the country's maximum-security prisons.

And for a while, they seemed to be keeping their word. In 2012 homicides fell almost by half.

On the other hand, gangs had been given a seat at the bargaining table. They now had officially recognized power. Countrywide, though the homicide count dropped, the menace remained. In 2012, the region where the Flores family lived registered more than two hundred disappeared; the next year it surpassed three hundred, and the following year nearly reached six hundred. Sometimes the disappeared would turn up dead, and sometimes they wouldn't turn up at all. La Colonia started reporting people vanished. The extortion rate skyrocketed. The *threat* of death, it turned out, was just as powerful as death itself.

By 2012, Wilber Jr. had mostly fallen out of contact. When he did call, it was to a neighbor's phone because the Flores family couldn't always afford to maintain theirs.

"We're fine, we're fine!" Esperanza would say, surrounded by her eight other children, all hungry. The harvest was bad that year. The family worried that they might run out of food; the portions got smaller every night. Ernesto and Raúl watched her lie cheerily.

"He has enough to worry about, up there all on his own," she would say after hanging up.

As things got worse in their country, the older Flores siblings spent more and more time imagining what it was like in the United States—where Wilber was, and what he was up to, and what was so bad, or causing him to be so selfish, that he was no longer sending back money.

Maricela, the eldest sister born between a bunch of boys, often felt lost in the shuffle of her siblings. At school she did her work and laughed at other kids' antics. It hurt when people said things about her brothers or her father, but she kept quiet. She, like the twins, was aware of her status as poor. But she also dreamed of going north, of making something of herself.

When she was eighteen and the twins were sixteen, her older brother, Ricardo, brought a friend over: Sebastian, a handsome eighteen-year-old. He stayed for lunch, and Maricela smiled when he spoke, shyly averting her gaze while helping her mother serve the tamales. She knew he was a lady-killer, and the fact that he wanted to talk to her made her feel like a star.

In part to slip out of her family's dire situation, she started hanging around with Sebastian. She texted him via her friends. They started to meet in person, flirting, and soon more. She was a virgin but perhaps, she felt, he was the one.

By the time she found out she was pregnant, he'd lost interest not only in sleeping with her but even in talking to her. She was terrified of her parents finding out. They should have used protection, she knew, but Sebastian had been careless about it, and she had been afraid to force the issue.

Maricela decided she'd have to hide for a while, to buy herself time to figure things out. A friend who lived a few towns over invited Maricela to stay with her family for a bit. So one day, at four months pregnant, she left school at midday, grabbed one of her family's two suitcases, and started packing.

"Where are you going?" her youngest brother Luis asked.

"Nowhere," she said. "To theater practice."

He shrugged. Within minutes she was a runaway. Later that same afternoon the school health promoter, who had given Maricela the pregnancy test that confirmed her fears, showed up at the Flores family door to deliver the news. Wilber Sr. was furious. Who was the father, and didn't his daughter know this was a sin? he raged. Esperanza prayed.

They didn't know how to track Maricela down. She

eventually sent a message that she was safe but wasn't ready to come home. She was too scared. But as the weeks passed, her parents imagined her belly growing with their first grandchild. What could they do now anyway? They hoped they could at least persuade her to marry the guy.

But that wasn't an option. Not only did Sebastian not call her or see her or send money, he was hanging around with several other girls. After a month Maricela was ready to listen to Wilber.

"You're our daughter. We want you to come back. We want to support you," he said. "Nothing will happen to you," he promised.

She went back home.

The day Maricela went into labor, Esperanza took her to the hospital where the twins had been born. Maricela gave birth to a little girl whom she named Guadalupe, or Lupita for short.

Back at home her siblings were eager to hold the baby. The only exception was Ricardo, the eldest. He didn't make eye contact with her and spoke to her only when necessary. Even though he was the one who had introduced her to Sebastian, he did everything he could, she felt, to make her feel unwelcome and ashamed.

Fifteen days after Lupita was born, Maricela still hadn't heard from Sebastian. She'd give him time—eventually he'd want to meet his daughter. When at last there was a knock at the door, instead of Sebastian, it was his parents. Maricela handed Lupita to her paternal grandmother.

"Sebastian left," his mother said.

"Left?" asked Maricela.

"*Al Norte,*" she said. To the North. Exactly fifteen days ago he'd climbed into a car with his *coyote* and left for the United States—just a few hours before Lupita was born.

The family was still struggling, and now there was a new baby in the house, another person to care for. Ernesto could go north, he thought in secret. If Wilber had survived the journey, and so had that asshole who'd knocked up his sister, he could, too. If he made it there, he knew he could make something of himself and support his family back home.

"You're crazy," Raúl told Ernesto. They had been spending more time either inside the house or up in the mountains, tending the animals and guarding the corn. Mornings and afternoons on the farm gave them time to dream, and the more Ernesto fixated on the faraway North, the realer it became.

Meanwhile, the gang boys at school kept pressuring Ernesto to join MS-13. They talked about the perks with cool ease, but what about the dead kid at the funeral with the gunshot through his head?

The North offered everything he wanted—success, belonging, respect, something better. He didn't want to leave, he thought in the quiet dark after Raúl nodded off, but at the same time he did.

In the late spring of 2013, someone hacked down Uncle Agustín's tree. It had been a giant tree, a *barillo* with a strong, sturdy trunk and smooth branches that spread into a thick canopy of leaves. Agustín was furious. Its fall, he said, had taken out a large swath of his coffee plantation, ruining much of the crop. The town gossiped, wondering who had knocked it down, and why.

By that time the Floreses were awaiting the May harvest, stretching their food to their last kernels of corn. Ernesto had officially decided to leave. One evening while his mother was cooking, he went into his parents' room to talk to his father. "Dad," he said. "I've been thinking about it, and I think I should go north."

His father was quiet for a few moments. "Why do you want to go?" he asked. "And how would you get there?"

Ernesto took this as a no. He didn't respond, just turned around and walked back into the main house.

The next night his father came to talk to him. "Okay, you can go," Wilber said. He'd done the calculations in his mind. They'd take out another loan. The family didn't want to lose another son, but they knew that it was probably safest for him.

Ernesto promised that he'd pay off the debt quickly and continue sending money home each month. It wasn't just his future he was concerned about, he insisted, but that of the whole family. He didn't mention that he was also hoping to escape the MS-13's persistent pressure on him.

Raúl knew that Ernesto had been thinking about going, but he was stunned into silence when Ernesto announced his plan. He stepped outside for air, hurt. Ernesto hadn't invited him, hadn't pleaded with him to come along. Raúl wouldn't so readily be able to leave Ernesto behind.

"You sure you want to go?" he asked later that night, in their room.

"Positive," Ernesto replied. They didn't talk any more about it.

The *coyote* would cost seven thousand dollars. He knew of people who'd gone on their own, with no *coyote,* no guide, and just enough cash for food, bus fare, and the occasional bribe. But Ernesto had barely ever left La Colonia, and now he'd have to cross El Salvador, Guatemala, and Mexico. They'd all heard horror stories, far worse than when Wilber had left seven years before: children raped in the desert, children dying of thirst, children run over by trains.

He, like Wilber, needed a guide. So they asked the most obvious person for money and for a *coyote*: Uncle Agustín. Wilber Sr. trudged to his house, took off his hat respectfully, and asked for a loan.

"No," Agustín told his brother-in-law.

Wilber thanked him and walked back home. He had a cousin, Erick, who also ran a *coyote* business. He would go to Erick instead, and borrow money from a loan broker in town. She'd loan them the money for the *coyote,* plus a few extra hundred in case of emergency. The interest, she said, would be 20 percent. Wilber put one of his plots of land up as collateral.

Ernesto would leave in two weeks' time.

In the following days everything looked different to Ernesto. He would miss every signpost, every view, every friend. Raúl most of all, though he wouldn't let on.

When just a week remained before his departure—one week to say goodbye—the family heard an ominous rumor. Something, it seemed, had led Agustín to believe that it was Ernesto who had cut down his tree.

Why would Ernesto have done it? And where had Agustín got the idea that he had? The twins decided one of their friends from school had started the rumor. They were jealous, perhaps, that Ernesto was going north and were trying to suck up to Agustín.

Someone spread more rumors that Ernesto and Raúl were gossiping about Agustín's livelihood, his gang connections, and his guns. The twins had certainly *heard* dark things about Agustín; he was rumored to have had people killed who stole from him. But Ernesto and Raúl insisted that they'd never said such things and they never would have.

Juan and Javier showed up at the Flores house. "Talking shit about my family?" Javier spat. He got close to Ernesto, as if he might hit him.

"We didn't say anything!" Ernesto insisted.

Raúl backed him up. "We wouldn't talk about your family!"

The cousins looked at them side-eyed, then walked out the door. This kind of bad-mouthing was treated as treason in the gang world. Agustín had always looked down on the twins' family, and now he had reasons—the tree, the alleged gossiping—to seek revenge.

Soon afterward Ernesto and Raúl were kicking a ball

back and forth along the road outside their house. Juan and Javier, heading toward town in one of Agustín's trucks, saw the twins and picked up speed. Ernesto and Raúl had to jump to the side of the road and flatten themselves against their house. As Juan and Javier tore by, they stared at Ernesto as if to say, *Next time, we'll mow you down.*

If Ernesto had had any doubts that he had to go north, they now vanished.

He went onto Facebook for some solace, posting:

> Feel so sad today cuz there's only a few days with my friends.

With his decision to go north now posted on his public feed, it wasn't just his few dozen "friends" who now knew of it, but anyone who cared to track him down.

Ernesto was to spend his last night in La Colonia in a safe house outside town, where he'd be picked up by his *coyota* the next morning. Raúl had decided to spend the night with his twin—the last time, surreal as it was, that they might ever see each other.

Late that afternoon the woman who ran the safe house got a call from Erick: *Tell them to leave,* he told her. She tracked the twins down at a friend's house. "Go hide up in the hills," she said.

It turned out that Agustín had found out Ernesto was leaving and was using a rival loan broker *and* a rival *coyote* company. Even though he'd refused to give Wilber a loan,

Agustín took them giving business to someone else as another slight. He was looking for Ernesto.

"We're changing the trip," the safe house woman explained to Ernesto. It was too dangerous to leave while Agustín and his boys were all lit up at him—they knew Erick's routes and might have them followed. So Raúl and Ernesto spent the night up on a hill, much as they had many times amid the corn, but this time more scared than ever—not of ghosts or thieves, but of Agustín's boys. They startled at every rustle and movement in the forest and didn't sleep at all.

"You have to go," Raúl acknowledged. It was no longer a choice.

The trip was postponed for more than a week, during which both Ernesto and Raúl stayed inside. Ernesto was a bona-fide target now—and Raúl, his identical twin, could easily be mistaken for him. Erick set a new date, with a new route, to leave town.

Ernesto once again took to Facebook:

> Ummm friends the 20th of this month I'm leaving
> I want you to know that I'm going to miss you.

"Don't do that!" Raúl said. But Ernesto couldn't help himself.

CHAPTER 4

It was late July 2013, and seventeen-year-old Ernesto's backpack was ready to go, packed with a few changes of clothes, a sweatshirt, a bar of soap, and a small cell phone that his father had bought him that, he said, would work in Mexico. "Don't tell them you have it," Wilber said. "You can use it to let us know how you are." Lastly he handed his son a plastic rosary, which they tied around his waist under his shirt for protection.

An aunt came over to say goodbye. "It's good he's going," she told Wilber. Earlier that day she'd been over at Agustín's. "I'd like to crush that boy's face in with a rock," she reported Agustín having told her. He'd slammed his fist into his palm by way of demonstration.

That last night Ernesto was restless. Raúl was, too, but he eventually nodded off, leaving Ernesto awake and alone.

Finally he slept, dreaming of his cousins and his family, set against the backdrop of a new life up north.

Just after dawn his mother woke him. He grabbed his backpack and hugged his parents and Maricela and baby Lupita goodbye, while fighting back tears and the jitters of departure. Raúl was still sleeping; Ernesto decided not to wake him. He walked out the door without even looking back.

Raúl awoke to find Ernesto's bed empty, his brother and his packed backpack gone. He took to Facebook.

> Today I feel so sad.

A friend commented:

> What's up man?

Raúl responded:

> It's that part of me, well like my best part, left since I'm a twin.

The family was relieved that Ernesto had made it out of town. Agustín didn't seem to know he was gone. But then again, if Agustín thought Ernesto was still around and was still looking for him, was Raúl at risk? Anyone could mistake Raúl for Ernesto. Or, the family reasoned fearfully, when Agustín's guys figured out Ernesto had left, what if they punished Raúl instead?

"I don't think you should go to school," Wilber Sr. said to Raúl, "just for a while," until things calmed down.

So Raúl stayed inside the house. He watched TV, ate, and played with Lupita, who by now was crawling. His other siblings were at school, and Ricardo was out in the fields, covering the twins' former work shifts.

Raúl was relieved, at first, to stay indoors. He wouldn't be able to look his friends in the face—they, he was sure, had spread the rumors. Plus, he was worried about running into his cousins or his uncle in the street. Would they try to run him over again? Would they crush his skull, as they had threatened to do to Ernesto, with a rock? Their threats could turn out to be just macho bluster—but what if they weren't?

In the frenzy of his brother leaving, he hadn't had much time to think about what it would be like to miss him. "When you're a twin, you share a heart" had long been Raúl's refrain, and though Ernesto had never said it, Raúl knew he felt it too. It was always funny to them how frequently they thought the same thing at the same time, or instinctively knew how the other was feeling. Pain, too—Raúl remembered that time the boys at school threw a rock at Ernesto, how he practically felt the shock of the blow on his own body. Without his brother, he felt alone.

He knew Ernesto could die on the road—among thieves and rapists and killers who preyed on migrants' vulnerabilities; the treacherous trains and buses; the Mexican *federales* and US border patrol hunting migrants like beasts; the fast-moving Angry River, the Río Bravo (what those north of the border call the Rio Grande); and that long stretch of desert into which so many migrants disappeared. He prayed for his brother's safety. Before he rose each morning, he could hear his parents praying, too: they prayed for everything and always expected the best, even in the face of the worst. The notion that bad things could happen to good people did not fit into their worldview. Raúl couldn't kick his certainty that the worst would happen.

Sad from missing his brother and bored from being stuck indoors, Raúl began to dissect how he had gotten here. He obsessed over what his friends—*ex-friends*—had done to his family. To make up these lies about Ernesto and rat him out to Agustín? Raúl knew for a fact that Ernesto had never talked shit about Agustín's business, the guns, the *coyotes*—his brother knew better than that. And the notion that he would cut down that tree? For all Raúl knew, the ex-friends cut down the tree themselves to frame Ernesto.

He vowed to get back at his *enemigos*. In his best moments, when he could think clearly and let God into his heart, he'd vow this: *If God gets me through this, I'll become someone—and my brother, too—and we'll show them.*

He changed his profile picture to a meme of white chalk against a black background:

SMILE: the enemy hates that.

The morning Ernesto had left, Erick had driven him without much talking to San Salvador. There they'd met the *coyota*, Sandra, a Mexican woman in her forties. She would accompany Ernesto across the Salvadoran–Guatemalan

46

border and up through Mexico to where he'd cross into the United States. Sandra was short, with long hair. She was younger than Ernesto's mother but, like her, sweet and smiling and maternal. She immediately put him at ease. On a crowded street in the center of San Salvador, he said goodbye to Erick and changed cars. He sat in the back, Sandra and their driver, a guy in his forties, in the front. But as they were pulling out, they noticed a car peeling out behind them.

Ernesto turned around and thought he recognized the car from La Colonia, as well as the guys in it. The car sped and swerved, as if trying to crash into them. One of the riders held a machete. Was it only his imagination that he recognized them? Ernesto's fear was overwhelming. His driver sped up, bobbed and dodged through traffic, and turned onto backstreets.

When it seemed they'd lost the car, they pulled over, and Ernesto and Sandra exited quickly, ducking into a small house that belonged to a friend of hers. They'd stay there "until things calmed down," Sandra said. They ate the thin Mexican tortillas that Ernesto called *lengua de gato,* cat tongues, for their floppiness, so unlike his mother's thick, soft tortillas with the thin crust. After a few hours they climbed into the car again and headed to the border.

As they got back on the road, the *coyota* and the driver, who seemed to have taken this route together many times before, began chatting about family and life. They didn't seem worried anymore. To Ernesto, the view outside appeared strange; hard to believe that this was still El Salvador. Even the trees looked different here, though he couldn't put his finger on why.

When it was fully dark and they were near the border, they stopped. They would take a bus from a small depot. Not a public bus but a large black private one, with which Sandra had some sort of arrangement. Ernesto sat down in an aisle seat with his backpack as the bus lurched into gear. At the Guatemalan border Sandra paid his entry—a tourist visa, she said, for her and her son. He fell asleep to the soothing whirr of the wheels.

After eight or so hours, they disembarked, Ernesto drowsy and squinting in the sunlight of some Guatemalan back road. This was the first step he had ever taken on land outside his own country. They walked for a while through forested hillside. Sandra seemed to know where she was going, and the isolation didn't worry Ernesto—he felt at home on foot in the dark among farmers like himself.

They came to a small house—the next stop, apparently, on this underground railroad. They were shown to a stuffy room that they would share. The bed looked too dirty to sleep in; Sandra took the couch; Ernesto, a hammock. He barely slept. The next morning they got on a nearby bus, this one public, packed with people and chickens and sacks of corn and coffee.

All day they rode through the mountains, dense and green, where indigenous people dressed in handwoven clothing worked the fields. No one on the bus talked much, and Ernesto just stared out the window. Another country.

This bus took them to the next bus. He wondered if he stood out as a foreigner, but no one seemed to notice him. Ernesto watched the world go by. He caught Sandra's faint murmurings here and there into a phone. He tried not to ask too many questions.

"Eat something," she said, handing him a piece of bread.

As the daylight dimmed they reached a gas station, where they waited for a car. No one showed up; the *coyota* was getting antsy, texting and calling again and again. "Stay here," she told him. "Don't move, and don't worry—I'll be right back." She hopped into a taxi.

But she didn't come right back. After about two hours of waiting on this dusty corner, Ernesto assumed he was abandoned. The phone his father had given him was still tucked in the bottom of his backpack—but who, besides his parents, could he call? And what would he say? *The lady left me here. All the money has been a waste.* He tugged at the rosary wrapped around his torso and waited.

Finally a van pulled up with a grumpy driver who shouted at him to get in. Ernesto hesitated, but the man knew his name and seemed to know where he was supposed to go. "Get in!" he barked again, and Ernesto did.

Inside the van a young man ordered Ernesto to take off what he was wearing. *I should never have gotten in here alone,* he thought, frozen to his seat. But then the young man pulled out a pile of clothes and dropped them onto the seat next to Ernesto.

"Put these on so you look Mexican," he said in a voice that didn't sound like a killer's—maybe he was just a tired guy doing his job.

Ernesto stuffed his old clothes into the bottom of his backpack.

The guy handed him a hat, too. "You're going to pretend to be the bus driver's assistant," he explained, "when you cross the border."

How could he know what a bus assistant in Mexico did, or what a Mexican kid would move or talk like? Ernesto wondered as the van pulled over. He got out and boarded a small, empty commuter bus. He pulled the hat low onto his forehead to shade his face, as the bus driver instructed him.

They pulled into the immigration station on the Guatemalan side of Ciudad Hidalgo. Ernesto held his breath, trying to appear calm as the immigration officer scanned his papers. The officer waved them on.

The bus wove up through Mexico, eventually slowing into the heave of morning traffic on the outskirts of a city Ernesto couldn't place. Ernesto hadn't eaten in almost a day. He worried once again that he'd been abandoned. But there, as the bus pulled over, was Sandra, cleaned up and smiling, waiting for him. He got into a taxi with her, and they rode through the massive metropolis of Mexico City, meandering through crooked streets until they reached a middle-class neighborhood where all the roads were named after birds.

They stopped at a two-story house in Las Aguilas, with plastered walls and a staircase inside; much nicer than Ernesto's home, with its bare bulbs and ragged curtains in place of doors. "Welcome to my house," Sandra said cheerily. He was about a thousand miles from home.

She lived there with her two daughters and a son, all a few years older than Ernesto. She showed him to the room where he'd be staying, then pointed him to the shower. It had been three days since he'd left home, but already, he saw in his reflection, he looked skinnier, older. The water was hot—a luxury. He scrubbed the grime from his skin.

Then he took out his hidden cell phone and called home.

The call from Ernesto was short, as he needed to preserve his airtime, so Raúl didn't get a turn to talk to him. He was relieved his brother was safe in Mexico, though he had figured as much. He'd know for sure if something had gone wrong. But Ernesto still had a long road ahead.

"He's fine," Maricela reported, "but he didn't sound good."

Meanwhile, rumors in La Colonia circulated that Agustín remained furious—about the gun gossip, the tree, and now, as he had finally learned, that Ernesto was headed north. The fact that Ernesto had left town seemed to affirm, in Agustín's mind, the boy's guilt. Raúl still hadn't left the house, except, occasionally, at night around the farm.

"Maybe," Wilber said to his son, "we should think about you going north, too."

Raúl didn't want to leave home for the uncertain, unfamiliar terrain up north. Couldn't he just go elsewhere in El Salvador for a while? But he worried that Agustín could use his connections to track him down. And anyway, he had nowhere else to go. Who would he live with, and what would he do? You couldn't live always looking over your shoulder.

The second time Ernesto called from Mexico, Raúl got to talk to him. "I'm nervous," he said. "I haven't gone outside. What if Agustín thinks I'm you?"

Ernesto was silent on the other end of the line.

"I'm wondering should I go, too?"

"No," Ernesto said.

Wilber took the phone. "We're thinking it might be better if he goes," he told Ernesto.

"It's too dangerous," Ernesto replied.

"We'll see." They said goodbye and hung up.

After Raúl heard his brother's voice, "it's like he changed his mind in a second," Maricela later recalled. "I think I should go," he told his dad.

Things were not calming down, and Raúl was still stuck inside the house. "It's better," Wilber agreed, "for you to be with your brother."

They arranged for a *coyota* from the same company that took Ernesto. In fact, it would be Sandra again, which gave the family some comfort. For safety reasons they'd take a slightly different route to Mexico City—if a *coyote* always travels the same network, he or she has a higher risk of being caught. Raúl would meet up with Ernesto in Mexico City. Together, they'd travel through the rest of Mexico and into the United States.

They'd have to borrow more money from the lender—another seven thousand dollars. That brought their total debt up to fourteen thousand dollars—with interest going up every week. As collateral they put up their second parcel of land. The debt amounted to more money than they had ever possessed, but certainly, the family reasoned, they'd be able to pay it off once the twins got to the United States. They would have their older brother Wilber Jr.'s help, once they got in touch with him. No one told Wilber Jr. that his twin brothers were going north until they were already gone. It had been a long time since he'd called. Raúl posted:

Something tells me, that I'm not coming back.

A friend of his, a girl, replied:

Noooo don't be like that!

Raúl responded:

Ernesto's going to be waiting for me in Mexico and from there we'll go, the two of us.

The night before he left, Raúl lay restless, listening to a pack of dogs howling into the dark. He felt sure the sounds weren't made by dogs at all but by spirits, warning of things to come. It had been nine days since Ernesto left.

The next afternoon Raúl got into a car with Erick, his mother, Maricela, and little Lupita. In his backpack was a gift from his father that, he promised, would keep him safe: *Prayers for El Niño Divino*, the Divine Child. They met up with the *coyota*, and he hugged his mother goodbye and looked at her in the eyes one final time. She was crying. Maricela bounced Lupita on her hip and told her brother to take care of himself.

"I'll bring them there," Sandra said, mother to mother. "Don't worry, I will."

CHAPTER 5

When Ernesto woke up in Sandra's house, she was gone.

"She left," explained Sandra's elder daughter. "Another trip from El Salvador." But she'd be back, the girl explained, in a few days, to take Ernesto to the northern border.

Ernesto called home.

Wilber gave him the news. Raúl left that very morning for San Salvador with Erick. "He's on his way."

Ernesto hadn't expected them to actually send Raúl north—not yet, anyway. His heart had skipped a beat when Raúl told him it might be best if he came, too. *What if Agustín thinks I'm you?*

What if something happened to Raúl on the road? Ernesto himself had been lucky making it this far; sending his double here, too, seemed to be testing fate.

At the same time he couldn't wait to see his brother. They hadn't even said goodbye.

Sandra was gone, and Raúl was gone, but Ernesto didn't put two and two together until Sandra called home. "I'm with your brother," she said. He let out a sigh of relief.

Mexico was hotter than El Salvador, and the heat made everything hazy and slow. He didn't mind being stuck in Sandra's house for a few more days—there was food, a clean bed, a shower, a TV, and the two sisters. He was especially drawn to the elder, Fernanda, with her long, thick hair; dark eyes; and brash confidence. They didn't ask him much about himself—they knew better, it seemed, than to pry.

A few days later the phone rang. Fernanda picked it up; it was Sandra. Ernesto, from his spot on the couch, heard the elder sister's voice go tense. He could tell something had gone wrong.

"What happened? What's wrong?" he asked. On the other line he could hear the frantic voice of the *coyota*.

Fernanda didn't answer him. She hung up the phone and disappeared upstairs.

From San Salvador, Sandra directed the driver along the back roads to the Guatemalan border. They crossed through a checkpoint, where an officer waved them through. They continued on into the thicket of Guatemala.

Sandra and the driver chatted like old friends, twisting the radio dial every now and again in search of a good song. Raúl just stared out the window. It was so quiet, the darkness outside shrouded the whole world from view. "Don't worry, just relax," Sandra said from the front seat.

"Nothing's gonna happen. We're fine." They drove on for a while through the blank stillness of the night, and Raúl tried to settle in. Suddenly Sandra gasped.

"*¡Dios!*" the driver whispered.

They had come to a roadblock, where a large black truck pulled out in front of them, and an officer in uniform motioned for their car to come to a stop. In the back of the truck were about ten men, all in uniforms, each clasping a machine gun between both hands.

An officer approached the car and bent over to talk into the window. "We're anti-narcotic officers," he said. "We need you to come with us."

Raúl stiffened. He didn't think they had drugs in the car, but he had no passport, and he assumed they would know from his accent that he was from El Salvador.

The driver pushed their car into gear, and they followed the truck off the main road into a dim thicket with no houses or traffic.

The same officer approached again, a photograph in hand. He held it up to Raúl's face. "Yep," he said, nodding, and flipped it around. "This is you, right?"

It was the photo of him, Maricela, and Ernesto wearing their best clothing at their ninth-grade graduation.

"Get out," the man ordered.

Raúl stepped out of the back seat, trembling. One of the officers grabbed him and threw him down, pressing his face into the ground with his boot. Raúl could hardly breathe. "Your uncle hired us," the man said, then bore down his boot even harder.

They weren't police at all. They were Agustín's hench-men. Or maybe they were both? The corruption ran too deep to tell.

They ordered Raúl to pull off his shoes and strip his pants and shirt. They yanked out his shoelaces and tied his wrists behind his back, facedown in the dirt, and did the same to the driver, who prayed out loud to God. Two men took Sandra away into the darkness; Raúl could hear her scream.

"Please," the driver pleaded. They took a metal pipe to his head and cracked him so hard that Raúl thought for sure he would end up dead.

Then they shook their guns toward Raúl and laughed.

This is where I die, he thought.

"Where's the money?" the guy asked. They rummaged through Sandra's stuff and found the cash.

"Please?" Sandra's voice piped up. "Leave us just a lit-tle, to get out of here?" Raúl was shocked she'd dare to ask, but they threw a few bills her way. Then, as quickly as they had appeared, the men retreated, their cars roaring into the night. It was now just the three voyagers again, tied up on a patch of dirt and far from anything, their money gone and, they noticed, the wheels of their car now missing. Sandra wiped her face, then untied Raúl and the driver. "Are you okay?" Raúl asked her.

She just handed him his clothes. They said nothing. With their shoelaces now broken, their shoes flopped open as the three of them trudged into the forest. They spent the night there, none of them sleeping much. Raúl knew it was sheer luck that he wasn't dead. He was certain that Agustín was trying to teach the family a lesson: *I'm boss. I'm in charge—run as far as you will, and I'll find you.*

The next morning, when the sun had risen, Sandra, Raúl, and the driver took stock: Dirty clothes, faces streaked with mud, a wily look in their eyes. The car was ruined, but the cell phone worked. Sandra called her daughter, pulling herself together. "A bunch of gangsters caught us," she said, her voice tight. "Don't worry, we're okay. We'll take the bus. We'll be there soon."

It took two days for the three of them to work their way north on buses, with not enough cash for anything but the tickets, not even food. Sandra soothed Raúl. "Don't worry," she said, "we're on our way, we're okay. We'll be there soon." She was trying to push onward as if nothing had happened. Raúl wondered if maybe this wasn't the first time she'd been attacked. As they moved into the thicker traffic of the big city, he was jumpy, every loud noise triggering a jolt through his brain.

When Raúl showed up at the door of the house in Las Aguilas, he was dirty and shaking, and his clothes were practically falling off in scraps. Ernesto grabbed Raúl and began, uncharacteristically, to cry. As if they'd swapped identities, Raúl just stood there, emotionless.

Sandra went straight to the kitchen and prepared some food. When the meal was ready, she called the boys in and went to clean herself up. Ernesto set a plate down in front of his brother: scrambled eggs, spicy sausage, and those thin tortillas.

Raúl ate slowly and hardly at all. Between labored bites, he told his twin what had happened. "It was Agustín," he said.

"How do you know?"

"They had a photo. The one from graduation."

Ernesto was silent for a while. It was his fault: he was the one Agustín wanted. He teared up again. He'd always taken care of his brother—he was the elder, after all, if even by twelve minutes—and now he'd failed. "Here," he offered softly. He gave his one change of clothes to Raúl.

They spent another few days in Las Aguilas while Raúl and the *coyota* got their energy back.

"You guys look *exactly* the same!" Fernanda said.

"No we don't!" they said in unison.

Seeing that it annoyed them, Fernanda teased them about how alike they looked for the rest of their stay. Raúl could see that Ernesto had a crush on her, for which he didn't blame him. But he was too tired to think about love.

After a few days they hopped a northbound bus with Sandra to Reynosa: the final border.

The Mexican border is punctuated by small cities like Reynosa: last stops and transit zones, places of free trade for the businessman, the migrant, the *coyote*, and the narcos. Most of the time Reynosa appears orderly enough, but beneath the surface, it roils. In the past decade violence and crime in Reynosa's state, Tamaulipas—and throughout Mexico—have increased.

By now, the migrants know all about the perils of the border. You move people; you move drugs; and more often than ever, you move them both at once. The face of the *coyote* is changing: no longer just a guide trying to make a buck while navigating people north but often a drug smuggler, too, or at least working for one—and almost always working with permission from the narco traffickers to move through their territory.

When the notoriously violent Zeta and Gulf drug cartels parted ways in 2010, Reynosa became a turf war battleground, leading to a major spike in homicides and other crime. *Los malos,* the bad guys, everyone calls them, shorthand for the *narcos*—but you avoid saying *narcos* out loud here. Even journalists and police, when they talk among themselves, tend to refer to them as *los malos.* As with El Salvador's *la violencia,* the violence, shorthand is safer.

Migrants aren't just wrapped up in the currents of the drug trade; they've also become its targets. In the past several years, the cartels have realized that migrants are lucrative marks. To reach the United States, Central American migrants have to move through more than six hundred miles of Mexico. That makes them potential drug mules. They often carry large sums of cash and have family waiting for them across the border who could pay a ransom. They flee the violence of the Northern Triangle only to pass through *another* war zone.

In August 2010, Los Zetas pulled seventy-two migrants from one of the northbound buses, shot them, then buried the corpses in and around the city of San Fernando. Dozens of suitcases arrived at the Reynosa bus terminal with no one to claim them.

The next year, in 2011, authorities uncovered 193 more bodies, often mutilated, scattered among clandestine graves around San Fernando. In 2012, the corpses of forty-nine people were uncovered in the adjacent state of Nuevo León. The majority of the dead, many of whose remains have yet to be identified, were migrants heading north.

They traveled fifteen hours out of the city and through northern Mexico, where the scenery changed from greenery to desert. Raúl silently prayed for no more bad encounters, while Ernesto looked steely-eyed out the window, braced for disaster. He felt he deserved it, after what had happened to his twin.

As they entered Reynosa they both noticed how poor it looked. The air was dusty, and children ran along the crumbling roadside without shoes. This was the last stop, the final crossing point before America.

The bus wove its way through the outskirts and into the city center, the roads thickening with traffic. Raúl could see Texas from here, right there across the bridge. Its proximity seemed ridiculous.

Sandra walked with them to a small garage with some mattresses on the floor and a card table. A few migrants, mostly young men and a few teenagers like them, were already inside.

Sandra wouldn't be crossing with them into the United

States, but she'd wait in Reynosa until she heard they were safely on the other side. She gave them each a hug. "Don't worry, you'll be just fine." She made them write down her number, just in case, before saying goodbye.

In the garage, Ernesto and Raúl claimed an empty mattress and lay there all day, close but not touching. Their fellow travelers intimidated them— Who knew what they were running from? Every so often more migrants were let in; the door was promptly shut behind them. By nightfall more than twenty people were packed into the little garage. There was food, at least; eggs, tortillas, beans. For two more days the twins lay on their mattress, waiting to be told it was time to move.

The single bathroom was upstairs. There was a faucet and a bit of soap. On the second day, Raúl went upstairs to wash up, leaving Ernesto in the packed room.

"Help me out back?" one of the *coyotes* asked him, the guy who, by his firm temperament and imposing stature, appeared to be the boss.

Ernesto obliged, jumping to his feet and following the man outside.

Twenty minutes later Raúl returned downstairs, cleaned up, but Ernesto was gone. After a while Ernesto walked back in through the door, ash white. He settled down onto the mattress in the fetal position and, despite the heat, pulled a sheet up over his head.

Raúl tried to get his attention. "What? What happened?" But Ernesto wouldn't look at him, and Raúl shrugged it off. Ernesto stayed silent for the rest of the night and through the morning; only the up-and-down motions of his chest beneath the sheet signaling to Raúl that he was alive.

"Tonight," one of the *coyotes* announced the third afternoon. They'd cross tonight. The atmosphere in the room shifted instantly: people prepared their bags and sat alert, mentally preparing for the road ahead.

Around midnight, the *coyotes* marched the group of about twenty migrants down to the river. The men pulled two inflatable rafts from the bushes and pumped them up with quick huffs. One of the *coyotes* ordered the first group to board the raft. "Get in," he said. Raúl and Ernesto stepped aboard, their weight sinking the soft bottom into the water. They could make out their own dark shapes against the river. On the other side, just as they'd been told, was the United States of America. The *coyote* pushed off, and they were afloat, on their way.

CHAPTER 6

The slow, muscular tug of that fabled river, the Rio Grande, acts as a liquid border wall between the United States and Mexico. Along the scrub of south Texas, everything sounds like a threat: wind rustling the palm fronds, a lizard skittering through the understory, the heavy flap of a low-flying hawk. Border patrol trucks cross like hunters. Thanks in part to environmentalist protest, the infamous border wall—a twelve-foot-high red metal fence—stops, for now, at Santa Ana's perimeter and starts up again on the other side. On opposite sides of the river, Mexico and Texas look just the same.

The history of the Rio Grande Valley is one of shifting borders, of hidings and crossings—this used to be Mexico, and before that, indigenous land. The whole of south Texas used to look like Santa Ana does now—the Sabal palms, Spanish moss, shallow swamps, hundreds of species of birds—before nearly all of the Rio Grande Valley was carved up as farmland, before the Rio Grande was both river and border, before the long chain of strip malls stretched along Highway 83, before the border wars and beheadings raged on the Mexican side, before the border patrol trucks scraped against the Texas dirt.

The call to "build the wall" along the southern US border is a misdirection: the desert border wall *already* stretches for roughly 650 miles of the two-thousand-mile southern border. It's not really one wall but rather dozens that, if one traces the border by car, appear and disappear abruptly against the agricultural fields and the sky. To connect all of them would mean building through massive swaths of harsh deserts and high mountains—at a cost the *Washington Post* estimated at tens of billions of dollars.

After the Rio Grande and the physical border wall, the next blockade migrants face is the US Customs and Border Protection (CBP) agents, who cruise the valley in their green and white vehicles.

And then, within a hundred miles of the border, are the checkpoints.

To reach the Falfurrias, Texas, checkpoint by car, you head seventy miles north on US 281, a highway that cuts through a vast desert rangeland. A sign along the road: SMUGGLING ILLEGAL ALIENS IS A FEDERAL CRIME. Border patrol agents man the checkpoint, clad in fatigues, black boots, and reflective sunglasses, holding tight to the leashes of German shepherds that sniff for drugs or bodies.

The migrants leave the road well before the checkpoint and head out into the desert's tangle of scrub and tumbleweed. It is hostile territory, but a weak spot in the US Customs and Border Protection's surveillance system. A person can walk for miles without seeing much but the occasional team of cattle, a low-set ranch house, or an unpaved road. Most migrants travel under cover of night, though this means stepping carefully to avoid snakes and thorns.

Ranchers come upon bodies, both fresh and decomposed, often enough. Each year the remains of hundreds of migrants are found along the southwestern border. Normally the bodies are desert-wrangled, burned and decomposed and picked over by scavengers, and they often carry no identification.

The county pays a local Falfurrias funeral home to intern the bodies in the Sacred Heart Burial Park. Most are dropped into unnamed graves.

They couldn't see much in the blackness apart from the stars. It wasn't so bad out here, thought Raúl, compared to what he had imagined during the days in the safe house. But ask anyone who's crossed the Rio Grande: the languid look of the river is a sham. Beneath the surface, the water rips fast and cruel. Before they left, the *coyotes* had told them that migrants like them had died making this crossing; Raúl couldn't help picturing corpses submerged in the water beneath him.

Once the raft bumped the Texas shore, the *coyote* hissed at them to get off. One by one the migrants scrambled up into the United States. As they came ashore the *coyotes* instructed them to run. The group struggled through dense brush as thorns ripped through the fabric of their pants. They ran for about an hour, then stopped to rest at a roadside spot with good cover. No one seemed to sleep. At about six in the morning, just as the sky was lightening, a couple of trucks arrived and picked the migrants up. They packed in and were taken to a safe house in one of the colonias, the small, poverty-stricken zones outside McAllen, Texas. The twins were so hungry, their stomachs cramped and groaned for food. The safe house operators handed out peanut butter and jelly sandwiches and water. The boys gulped them down.

They waited. On the night of the second day, they packed into trucks again and headed for the desert. There, they'd walk overland, passing around the Falfurrias immigration checkpoint, and meet up with a truck on the other side for the drive to Houston. The twins would call Wilber from there.

That night twelve rode in the front cab and even more in the truck bed, huddled in silence. About an hour north, the driver pulled over. But as he cut the headlights and the migrants began to get out, a border patrol car approached, flashing.

The world went silent inside the twins' heads, as everyone scattered in different directions. Ernesto lurched into action, Raúl following close behind. They ran and ran until the lights were far behind them, then crouched in the night and caught their breath.

They looked around and spotted Edy, a nineteen-year-old from Honduras, with whom they'd exchanged only a few words. Everyone else had vanished into the desert.

The trio set out walking, with no idea where they were heading but knowing they needed to move.

"We're close. Don't worry. We got this, guys. We're getting there," Edy said as they hiked. His insistent optimism soothed the twins.

"Think about it—we're so close. Close to our dreams, man, close to reaching our destiny," Edy continued, his comforting voice spinning tales in the darkness.

In spite of his pep talks, however, Edy groaned every few steps—he had fallen and twisted his ankle on something. He soldiered through the night, not wanting to slow the group down.

When the sun came up, they rested beneath a mesquite tree, desperate for shade and to keep from being spotted. They scanned the horizon. Had they been going in circles? *Where were they?*

Ernesto rummaged through his backpack for the phone. He turned it on: two bars of signal. "I think it works!" he told Raúl.

He tried texting Sandra: "We're lost."

Within moments his phone pinged with a message from her. The three boys laughed in relief. "Don't worry, you'll be okay. Where are you?" read the text.

"In the desert."

Pick a direction and keep walking, she told them. Once they got past the US Customs and Border Protection's station in Falfurrias, she instructed, there'd be a car there waiting for them.

They'd make it to a road as long as the boys could mark a straight line in one direction, ideally north. They picked a direction and tried to keep straight.

"You're at the last step," she wrote. "You're so close."

These messages lifted the boys' spirits for a while, and they walked with renewed confidence in spite of their thirst and the empty terrain.

"I can't wait to get a job," Edy said. He was planning to stay in Houston, where his dad lived. "Construction, restaurant, whatever—I'll get any kind of job. Think about it— How great will that be?"

The three spent another aimless night forging a pathway through the arid rangeland. During the day they hid out; at night they walked.

Raúl's shoes were coming apart, the stitching unraveling. Finally the soles came undone and flapped with each step, exposing his feet to the spiny brush. How would he go on like this, half barefoot?

"Here." Ernesto yanked off his shoes. "Take mine."

Ernesto pulled Raúl's destroyed shoes onto his own feet and undid the laces, winding them around the bottom of the soles to hold the halves together, then tied them as tightly as he could.

"Thanks," Raúl said.

Ernesto grimaced to make sure Raúl knew he was annoyed at him for letting this happen.

That second night, Ernesto insisted on walking ahead,

though he had no more idea where he was than the other two did.

"We got this, boys," Edy kept saying. "The last step. We're almost there." The twins nodded and kept moving.

Around three in the morning, the stars bright in the sky, Raúl heard a sharp yipping sound behind him. *Evil spirits,* he thought, *on the hunt again.*

The noise repeated, louder. They all stopped. "Fuck," Edy said. "Coyotes."

They walked faster. Every bark felt like an electric shock.

They found a low mesquite tree and scurried up into the slim branches, hurling rocks toward the sounds, until eventually the animals lumbered away.

The next day their thirst became unbearable. It scratched their throats. Occasionally they came across a cattle trough and drank, first skimming green muck off the water's surface. The water tasted terrible, but it soothed their throats.

Maybe this was where they'd die, Raúl thought. At least they'd die together. Sometimes he prayed for the border patrol to come and find them—though then they'd be sent back to El Salvador and would likely die all the same. No, they had to make it to Houston and then on to California.

"I wonder what the others are doing," Raúl said. The guys from their migrant group, he meant. Had they been caught, or were they also lost in the desert? Or worse?

Edy's limp had grown more pronounced, but he kept up the positive talk. "Just a little more, brothers, just imagine how close we are. Reaching our dreams!"

By this time, though, Edy was sick. His stomach hurt, and as they walked, he had less and less to say. They figured he might be dehydrated, or maybe it was something in the water they drank. Normally he took medication every day, but he'd been off it for a week now. They needed help. Sandra in Mexico wasn't of much use. So Ernesto texted Wilber Jr. They were in his territory now, after all: "We're in the desert in Texas," he wrote. "Me and Raúl. We're lost. We have no food or water." They didn't get a reply. He texted the same thing to his sister Maricela.

Finally, in the distance, they spotted a house. It appeared empty. They moved toward it cautiously.

The door was unlocked, so they stepped inside and crept into the kitchen. They turned on the faucet and took turns sucking water straight into their mouths. They'd seen a hose outside, and Ernesto went out to fill their water bottles. They were trespassers, but they were desperate. Raúl apologized to God, then began rummaging through cabinets stocked with bread, rice, and cans. He began pulling them from the shelves.

Just then a man walked into the kitchen.

Raúl saw him first and immediately put his hands up. Edy startled and did the same. Eyes wide and hands in the air, the boys backed away from the counter, trying to show they meant no harm. The man's wife walked in, seeming not all that surprised at their presence.

"Who are you guys?" the man asked in Spanish.

"We're coming from Mexico," Edy said. "We're sorry. We're so sorry. But we're lost."

"Don't be scared," he said. He told them to call in "the other guy." Raúl yelled for his brother to come inside. Ernesto, too, put his hands in the air.

71

The man sat them down at the table and poured them glasses of water, then, once the boys emptied them, refilled them with juice. He put a stack of bread in front of them. They ate it, slice by slice.

"Don't worry," he said. "You just gotta walk that way." He indicated a direction. "If you go that way"—he pointed in another direction—"you'll hit a big road with an immigration station, and you want to avoid that."

The boys nodded as the man pointed in the right direction again. "Thank you," Ernesto said. He retied his shoelaces around the broken soles, and the boys took off walking.

They trudged on, feeling better. As night fell, they heard nothing but the sound of their feet crunching through the scrub. Lost in thought, Ernesto tripped on something and fell. He reached his hands out to catch himself, but as he hit the ground, his hands landed in a soft mass that collapsed into a wet mess beneath him.

As he pushed himself up, he realized he'd fallen onto a human body.

He screamed.

Raúl ran up behind him. They could see in the dim moonlight that the corpse was headless.

Ernesto fell backward onto the ground away from it, shaking and hyperventilating. A migrant, alone and decapitated, in their very path. "I touched it," he whispered. "I touched it with my own hands."

Raúl and Edy soothed him, but Ernesto couldn't speak for a long time.

They kept walking, then rested at dawn and through the

heat of the next day. While the two others slept, Ernesto forced his eyes to stay open. He couldn't shake the feeling of death on him. When he finally nodded off, he dreamed that two men were chasing him to cut off his head.

He awoke with a start.

A text popped up on the screen. "Okay, *está bien.*" It was their brother Wilber.

CHAPTER 7

Finally they came to a road. Through the darkness they saw cars flying in both directions. Could they pass without being seen? They hid in the scrub. A light flashed over them. A truck was speeding their way.

Edy, despite his weak stomach and ankle, took off running again. But not the twins. They wanted to follow Edy, but their feet wouldn't move. Ernesto's shoes were torn to bits, and they were hungry and thirsty and rendered inert by everything that had brought them here.

"Stop," they heard in Spanish. It was the border patrol, *la migra.*

"Don't move!" an agent shouted.

They stood there, hands in the air, eyes heavy and resigned. Raúl braced himself to be punched and kicked into submission. "What are your names?" he asked in twangy

Spanish. He turned the boys around, patted them down, and cuffed them. More trucks had pulled up.

"Where are you from?" the agent asked. "Where are you going?"

The twins answered in unison. "California."

The agent nudged Ernesto into his truck. He passed Raúl to another agent. They were separated.

"Don't worry," Ernesto called to Raúl. "I'll see you when we get there." He wasn't sure where "there" was, but he didn't want Raúl to be too scared.

Inside the truck, Ernesto's agent filled out some paperwork and handed him two bottles of water and a packet of crackers. Ernesto sucked down the water. They were caught, but they weren't dead.

"How old are you?" the agent asked.

"Seventeen."

So they counted as "juvies," as the border patrol called them—under eighteen, paperless, and parentless. The agents knew there were thousands of kids like them, and the numbers kept rising. By the end of September 2013, 24,668 minors would have been taken into federal custody with the Office of Refugee Resettlement. For all of 2013, fully 93 percent of these "juvies" came from the Northern Triangle. The twins were just two among thousands.

In another truck, separated from his brother, an agent told Raúl, "You boys are lucky I found you when I did. We just found five dead bodies not too far from here." He put the truck in gear, and drove.

Raúl figured they were headed to the border to be

dropped off in Mexico. Perhaps after that they could try to swim back across on their own. But then what?

After all that, Raúl thought, they might just be sent right back home.

In fact, they weren't. The agents took them to the immigration station to be fingerprinted and questioned. There the twins, thankfully, were reunited. Being under eighteen mattered: if they'd been over, they would have been put into an adult detention center and ordered deported, likely without even seeing a lawyer. Instead they were put in a "youth friendly" shelter overseen by the United States' Office of Refugee Resettlement (ORR).

First they were sent to the *hielera,* or icebox—the immigration holding tank, the official limbo zone of the US immigration system.

The icebox was a cold, windowless room, packed with about thirty other young men and boys. They shared one toilet, and going to the bathroom meant doing so in front of everyone. There were no beds or mattresses, and it was too difficult for everyone to lie down on the concrete floor all at once, so they took turns. Immigration gave out juice boxes and cookies every now and then. The air conditioner remained cranked up seemingly as high as it could go, in spite of the inmates' quiet suffering.

Immigration advocates say that the cold temperature is intentional, a tactic used to break the spirits of immigrants who, they hope, will opt for voluntary departure—that is, agree to be sent home.

76

A 2008 internal border patrol memorandum asserted that immigration detainees should not be held in *hieleras* for more than twelve hours before being released to an official detention center. After all, there are no beds or showers. But the reality (according to a report by the American Immigration Council) is that they are often held longer—an average of four days. In 2015, a US district court judge ruled that the Department of Homeland Security (DHS) must release children from their custody to that of the Office of Refugee Resettlement within seventy-two hours.

Conditions in *hieleras* are widely known to be grim and inhumane. In June 2014, the ACLU and other human and immigrant rights groups filed an administrative complaint against US Customs and Border Protection, outlining evidence of physical, verbal, and sexual abuse—as well as the withholding of food, water, and medical care—of unaccompanied minors in the *hieleras*. A few months after the twins were first detained, photos of children in these *hieleras* were leaked to the press. The images of dozens of children locked in windowless rooms revealed the deplorable conditions to which they were subjected. The photos spurned outrage on all sides for the poor treatment of minors within our borders.

First separately, then together, Raúl and Ernesto were taken from the miserable *hielera* and interviewed by an immigration officer. She asked if they had anyone in the United States they could call.

Wilber picked up after a few rings. "Who is this?" he

asked suspiciously. Despite their texts from the desert, he didn't totally believe it was them.

"Ernesto and Raúl. Immigration has us," said Ernesto. Silence.

"Hello?" Ernesto said.

"You're here? Seriously? How are you?"

"Hungry," he said. "But we're okay."

The officer took the receiver, asked Wilber a series of questions, and jotted down his information. The twins knew Wilber didn't have papers. Had they just gotten him in trouble with the authorities?

They waited in the *hielera* for three days or so; it was hard to mark the passage of time since the lights were always on. Then they were put into a car with four other boys, sure once again that they were being taken to the other side of the border. But soon they were pulling up to a two-story white clapboard house with a sign on the gate: SOUTHWEST KEY PROGRAMS.

What *was* this place? they wondered. At the front desk they handed over their belongings. They took showers and were given a change of clothes—jeans, shorts, T-shirts, and sneakers. They were given medical tests and vaccinations. They were left in isolation for three days, just the two of them in a room, lying around in the mornings, pissing into cups, getting their blood drawn.

Southwest Key Programs, they soon understood, was a shelter. When they were finally released from isolation, they found themselves, to their surprise, among about two hundred minors, mostly teens from Central America like them.

They were put into a room with two sets of bunk beds

that they shared with two boys from Guatemala. It didn't seem so bad in here. Better than in the *hielera*.

The staff woke them up at five-thirty a.m. to take showers and do chores. Rooms were kept neat and orderly for daily checks. During the day they attended English classes; played soccer; and met occasionally with their counselor, Gerardo.

Ernesto looked forward to his meetings with Gerardo. He told him things he'd never told anyone before, not even Raúl. His dreams had been getting worse and worse—like the recurring dream with a headless man chasing him down, trying to strangle him. In the daytime Ernesto began to suffer from panic attacks, and Gerardo helped him calm down. "Breathe," he'd say. "Deep breaths." With each inhale, Ernesto was to focus on calming, and with each exhale, he'd repeat out loud something bad that had happened, as if he were releasing it into the air around him.

"My uncle wanted to kill me."

"My brother was kidnapped, and it was my fault."

"I fell onto a body—I can still feel it on my hands."

"What happened that day in Reynosa . . ."

After sessions like that, he could sleep a little. But the following day the cycle would start over again.

Raúl noticed that Ernesto wasn't doing so well. He was glad Ernesto had his counselor. But why wouldn't he talk to him?

The Southwest Key facility in San Benito, Texas, is part of a lucrative federal contracting industry. Contracts are awarded to nonprofit agencies for the short-term housing of unaccompanied minors.

Before 1997, unaccompanied minors like the Flores twins had been detained along with adults in prisonlike detention facilities. That put them at obvious risk. In 1997, an agreement known as the Flores Settlement (no relation to the twins) laid out new requirements for child-appropriate facilities. It allowed for children to be released, when possible, to trusted adults in the United States pending their immigration proceedings in court.

In 2003, the Department of Homeland Security changed the rules. Unaccompanied minors were put in the care of the US Department of Health and Human Services (HHS)—specifically, the ORR—which meant the government agency that was attempting to deport children was no longer also in charge of their day-to-day care.

These youth detention facilities were now run by outside contractors, all nonprofit agencies like Southwest Key. But in spite of their nonprofit status, youth shelters are often a big business. The year the Flores twins crossed the border, HHS budgeted $175 million for the Unaccompanied Alien Children Program, more than 80 percent of which went to the shelter costs through federal contracts. In the fiscal year 2017, the ORR's Unaccompanied Alien Children (UAC) budget was approximately $1.32 billion, up more than $373 million from 2016.

Southwest Key is one of the largest UAC contractors. Though it is a nonprofit, it looks a lot like a private prison company in its reliance on high-priced federal contracts.

In some cases former prison guards actually work in the shelters.

Abuse is depressingly common. A 2014 *Houston Chronicle* exposé reports 101 cases of sexual misconduct between 2011 and 2013, with unaccompanied minors in custody in New York, Illinois, Texas, and Florida; the alleged abuse was often accompanied by threats if these incidents were reported. The *Chronicle* reported that "In the hands of local police and prosecutors, criminal cases have crumbled because of sloppy detective work [and] communication gaps with federal officials." As a result, very few perpetrators have served jail time, and none of them were prosecuted under a 2008 federal law designed specifically to protect children in custody from child abuse.

When the budget is broken down, the total cost of detaining each child has, since the initial 2012 surge of unaccompanied minors, totaled between two hundred and five hundred dollars per night. Profits have been big: in 2014, the Southwest Key CEO made $659,000—all of this at the expense, of course, of these young migrants.

The Flores twins stayed at the Southwest Key facility for more than two months. There, a social worker finally explained what was happening to them. They had entered the country illegally, she said, so they might be deported—but not before first going to court and talking to a judge. They could try to find a lawyer to fight their case, though that might cost money. If the judge did not accept their plea to stay, they would be deported. Meanwhile, they'd stay at Southwest Key. If family in the United States was willing to take them in, they could be transferred out of the facility to live with them.

"But," the woman warned, "this does not mean you have permission to stay in the United States for good. You still have to go to court."

The social worker explained the release process to Wilber Jr.: He would be background-checked, and if they found him fit to be a sponsor, he would have to pay the plane fare for the boys to travel to his city, as well as for a social worker to accompany them on the journey. He would be responsible for making sure they were fed, clothed, and housed; that they were safe; that they enrolled in school; and most important, that they made it to their court date.

She added, "And if you don't have papers, don't worry—this will not impact your immigration status."

Wilber took the social worker at her word. Within a few days he started the process to become the twins' guardian.

Once a week Ernesto and Raúl got to make a fifteen-minute phone call home. They alternated between calling Wilber and calling their parents. Fifteen minutes went quickly. Gerardo sometimes let Ernesto make special phone calls home during their sessions. Talking to Esperanza was the most soothing for him and also the hardest of all. "I'm okay, don't worry," Ernesto would say. But she didn't believe him; he could tell. Likewise, the twins didn't believe her when she insisted everyone was safe back home. They worried that Agustín might go after their family to punish them.

Meanwhile, they made a few friends at the shelter, who, like their old classmates, referred to them as "the twins," *los gemelos*. They didn't share much about their past, instead focusing on video games, gossip, and what was for dinner that day. The food was terrible—slop on a tray; nothing like what they were used to eating at home.

Occasionally the kids with good behavior were taken out on field trips. One night it was to the movies; the Flores twins had never been to a movie theater before. They loved the cool, dark room and the chairs you could sink into, to stare up at the big screen. They had no idea what the film was called, or what exactly was happening, since it was in English. Something about a boy and girl falling in love. The popcorn was delicious.

They went to the park in town from time to time to kick the ball around. Once, they heard a commotion and turned: a man was shouting that he didn't want his own kids playing with a bunch of immigrants. Eventually the guy collected his own children and drove away.

The twins wanted out of Southwest Key as fast as possible. Their debt was climbing, and every day in there was another day they weren't earning money to pay it back. They called Wilber every other week, asking for an update, hoping he hadn't changed his mind about letting them come live with him.

They'd never been on a plane before. As the wheels lifted off the tarmac, the Flores twins gripped their armrests and held their breaths. Flying seemed miraculous. The brothers whispered to each other, drank soda, and stared out the window. The woman from the shelter hardly spoke to them.

Wilber was waiting for them when they landed at San Francisco International Airport. At first the twins didn't recognize him. After seven years Wilber was like a different person: new clothes, newfound swagger. He didn't look much like his twins' brother. His face was more drawn, less wide-eyed—the effects, perhaps, of being on his own up north. At five foot six, he was simultaneously brawny and trim. He walked with confidence, and his front teeth were ringed by gold caps that gave his timid smile an actual glint.

They exchanged stiff hugs and laughed uneasily. After Wilber signed some papers, the shelter staff released them officially into his care.

Wilber had a girl with him. "This is Gabby," he said. She had a red rinse in her hair and thick black glasses.

"Hi," said Ernesto.

"Nice to meet you," said Raúl.

Wilber had taken the day off work to fetch the twins in San Francisco, about an hour north from where he lived in San Jose. The past two months he'd taken on all the Sunday shifts he could at the landscaping company where he worked in order to pay for their tickets—this was his first break in weeks. He noted how skinny his brothers looked—this upset him and, also, it was now his responsibility to feed them.

They rode the train to San Jose; then at the station they hopped into his car and at Wilber's request buckled their seat belts. The car rode high off the ground and had leather seats that were smooth to the touch. The Flores family had never owned a car. Wilber pulled into a parking lot and left the twins inside the car. He and Gabby came back a few minutes later, paper bags in hand. "Burgers," Wilber said. Delicious.

Wilber's working-class San Jose apartment—their new home—was nicer and more modern than any house they'd ever been in. He showed them around. It had two bedrooms: one for him and one for his roommate and his roommate's girlfriend. The twins would sleep on the couch.

They all spent that first afternoon watching TV. They didn't know what to say to one another. Wilber could see in their faces that they'd been through the wringer. He knew how bad the journey could be, but he didn't ask any questions. They'd survived, and to keep pushing forward, these things were best left undiscussed. Maricela had already told him what had gone down with Uncle Agustín.

Wilber had followed the news from El Salvador since he left, seeing the pictures of dead bodies, the statistics, the way the police covered their faces now, so the gangs wouldn't know who they were. He read stories on Facebook by Salvadoran friends and coworkers. Two friends of his had gone back to El Salvador from the United States. Both had been killed. If you returned to El Salvador, you were an unknown, a *desconocido*. The gangs knew who belonged and who didn't, and a new guy rolling into town with nice clothes was assumed either to have money, or to be a part of a rival gang, or both. Wilber wasn't surprised that this plague of violence had made its way to his family. His country, as far as he could tell from this distance, was falling apart.

Still, seeing his little brothers grown up and no longer scrawny little boys made him miss home: the fresh smell of the hillsides, the sweet burn of brushfires, his mother at the stove. When he left home six years ago, he had been so preoccupied with the dream of what awaited him in the United States that he hadn't really considered that he would very possibly never return.

Things don't always work out as planned. Right when he got to California, aged seventeen, he had enrolled in high school, which he'd assumed would just be a stepping-stone to college. But without English, US high school was harder than he'd thought it would be. Plus, though he had a place to stay—on the couch of friends of the family—financial pressures kicked in quickly. He wanted to pull his weight in the household, and he had his six-thousand-dollar debt to pay off. Feeling sure that he'd reenroll once things stabilized, he quit school and got a job in landscaping, working on the yards and gardens of Silicon Valley's wealthy homes and businesses. They paid him in cash every other week—more cash than he'd ever had. But life in the United States was a nonstop grind. He moved out and rented a room in a house—that was a monthly bill. He needed a car. Strong shoes, work gloves, gas and insurance for the car—he was always behind. But he was diligent about sending money home to work off his debt. He paid it off a few hundred dollars at a time, finishing within two years, never letting the interest overtake him.

The twins would have to go to work as he had—he understood this before they even arrived. But shelter rules said otherwise. "They'll have to go to school," the woman from the shelter had explained in her Tex-Mex Spanish. "They can't work."

So who was going to pay their debt?

"How much do you owe?" he asked them over burgers.

"Fourteen thousand dollars," Raúl said.

"When we left," said Ernesto, shaking his head. The sum, they knew, had compounded, or increased with interest, in the three months since they'd left. They weren't sure by how much.

Wilber took a bite, nodding silently. He loved them, and had missed them. Now their debt, it seemed, was his. "I'll help you guys," he'd told them over the phone. But now, hearing the impossible sum they owed, he didn't repeat his offer. They'd figure out their own paths forward, in time.

CHAPTER 8

The idea that unauthorized immigration into the States is increasing is a myth. From 1990 to 2007, the number of undocumented people rose steadily from around 3.5 million to 12.12 million, but in 2009, it *dropped* (owing largely to the economic recession) to approximately 11.3 million. It has stayed relatively steady ever since. But immigrant demographics have changed. In 1990, approximately 525,000 undocumented people living in the United States had come from Central America. By 2011, that number spiked to 1.7 million.

Another myth is that immigrants like Wilber do not pay taxes that contribute to the community. In fact, taxes are taken out of immigrants' paychecks; they pay sales tax on groceries and cars. When undocumented immigrants use fake or borrowed Social Security cards, they are paying into the real Social Security benefit pool—benefits that they will never receive. They pay property tax. In 2012, according to the American Immigration Council, the undocumented paid $11.8 billion in state taxes alone.

Undocumented immigrants may use public services like schools, roads, and public hospitals, but they do not qualify for benefits like welfare, food stamps, subsidized housing, or health insurance (even under the Affordable Care Act)—even though these are resources they frequently and desperately need.

Wilber worked hard, paid his rent on time, paid his car payments on time, and stayed out of trouble. By the time the twins arrived, he was just starting to feel settled, to build a life he could be proud of. He had Gabby, who was Salvadoran, too, though she'd been born in the United States and spoke perfect English. Gabby's Chihuahua, Nicky, lived with her family inside their house. Nicky relaxed Wilber. Anytime he was having a bad day, the dog's antics lifted his spirits. Gabby was finishing up her high school credits at the local community college, after which she'd enroll as a full-time college student. Wilber wanted to enroll in college, too, though he couldn't, just yet, because of work. He also wanted to marry Gabby if things kept going well. Gabby was a citizen, and if they got married, perhaps he could get papers. But, Wilber reasoned, "you have to get married for love."

Wilber bought Ernesto and Raúl new clothes at the local mall. Ernesto picked out a Bob Marley T-shirt with an image of him dragging on a joint. Back home they had dressed more conservatively, with collared shirts tucked into straight-legged pants. Here, the styles were different—

skinny jeans, fitted sweatshirts, oversize high-tops only barely laced. It was like what Wilber wore—and not unlike gangster garb back home. When Wilber saw the Bob Marley shirt, he just laughed. The shopping trip drained him of all that month's extra cash.

He was happy to see the twins, but their arrival was also a game changer. Just when things had started to stabilize and he was thinking about going back to school, his brothers appeared, needing food, a place to sleep, and clothes. They were his blood and they needed him, so of course he'd help them, but damn.

Wilber secured another day off to enroll the twins in the local school, Westmont High. He gathered all their documents—birth certificates, release papers from Southwest Key, vaccination documents—and walked into the main office. But since the twins didn't speak English, they wouldn't be able to graduate on time. The administrator suggested another school that had a program for English learners.

Wilber didn't argue. The US immigration system required them to register in school, but that was proving complicated. It would be a while before he could get another day off to try the other high school. If they couldn't go to school yet, Wilber reasoned, they should at least help pay the rent and start sending money home. His boss said he might need a few extra hands. So in their second week in California, the twins began mowing lawns, trimming hedges, and pulling weeds from the gardens of mansions.

Ernesto and Raúl made nine dollars an hour and, for two months, worked whenever the boss texted that he could use them. The money they earned went to food and rent, and whatever was left over they sent home: $100, $150, every couple of weeks when they had some extra to spare.

"Can you send more?" Maricela wrote over Facebook.

Their debt had started at fourteen thousand dollars. By the time they set foot in the United States, it was sixteen thousand dollars. Of the money the boys did send home, hardly any of it even went to the debt because the family needed it to eat. The land that Wilber Sr. had first put up as collateral had been valued, loosely, at around sixty thousand dollars.

To lose the land would mean losing the family's livelihood, their food source. For Wilber Sr., the land also signified his very purpose in the world, entwined with his own origin story.

The twins' father had been born to a mother who had been just fifteen; his father had run away. Afraid and heartbroken, Wilber's mother gave birth to him in a cornfield. She cut the cord, left him there in the dirt, and then like his father, ran away. Her sisters found the baby. Their own mother had just given birth a few months before, so Wilber's grandmother nursed both of them.

After the second grade, he quit school to farm full-time. At twelve, his father, whom he'd never met, showed up. He had another family by then, and he wanted Wilber to come and live with them. It quickly became clear that Wilber had been brought there just to work. While the other siblings went to school, Wilber was in the fields. One of these siblings was Graciela, Agustín's wife.

Wilber felt used. Finally he ran away to the forest. But there, his story went, the spirit of an old woman appeared and told him she'd buried a treasure on the mountain. She told him he could find it beneath a pine next to a huge rock. He went there and dug up a stash of money—enough, he said, to purchase the land and start his own family.

Who knows what was true? Wilber Sr. told the story of his life as this sort of parable. The moral of this tale: his land was something he'd come to through both patient suffering and divine intervention.

Now his sons' debt was putting it all in jeopardy, and Wilber Sr. felt uncharacteristic doubt. Not Esperanza. "God will find a way," she insisted. She lit a candle on the altar.

To Maricela, this wasn't about God—it was about numbers, a sum of money that needed to be paid off quickly.

Ernesto and Raúl received a letter from immigration court. Their case had been transferred from Texas to California. They were due at the San Francisco Immigration Court in February 2014: in less than two months' time.

By December 2013, the boys had been living with Wilber in San Jose for two months. When they weren't at the landscaping job, they were at home, worrying over their debt and their court cases and hiding away in the dark apartment in case neighbors saw them and snitched to *la migra*.

Nights were the hardest. Raúl thought of the barking dogs the night before he left La Colonia, the guys with the photo on the side of the road. Were the dark spirits here in California? He frequently spotted a flash across his wall, or felt a cold chill come over his body. He waited and prayed until these went away. Ernesto didn't see spirits, but when Raúl told him, he believed him.

Ernesto's sleep was worse now, and in San Jose, he had no counselor to help him. Almost nightly he had suffocating dreams. He'd be in a bus, or out in the desert, or in the forest back in El Salvador, and a dead man would rise and chase him. The first night he had that dream in San Jose, he woke up screaming. He opened his eyes and saw Wilber above him, shaking him.

"What's wrong? What's wrong?" Wilber asked.

Ernesto brushed him away. "I'm fine, sorry." He rolled back over.

"You sure you okay?" asked Raúl, after their brother left.

"I'm fine!" Ernesto said, and yanked the covers over his head.

Once the dreams became a pattern, Raúl would just roll over and ignore the screams. He didn't ask about what Ernesto was dreaming about. Clearly that dead body he had fallen on had affected him, or maybe it was the stress of the upcoming court date, or the fear of gangs from home. It used to be that Raúl could just look at Ernesto and know his thoughts, but perhaps the twins were losing their special powers up north.

• • •

Around the holidays Wilber began to talk about moving. Gabby was starting school again in Oakland. If they all moved to Oakland, about an hour north, they could rent a larger place along with her mom, Rosalinda. Wilber would have to commute to work an hour and a half every day, each way, but the rent would be cheaper, he figured.

Christmas was one of their last days in San Jose, spent at a barbecue in a parking lot across town, grilling meat and eating *pupusas* with a dozen or so other Salvadorans. They missed the nativity scene their mother always set up on the home altar, missed the songs in church and the fireworks at night. But they had something to look forward to: a new apartment, maybe even school.

Oakland was busier and, to the twins, felt poorer than even La Colonia. Urban poverty was different; it was on display for everyone to see. Homeless people walked the streets, people did drugs out in public, there was litter everywhere, and sometimes they heard gunfire. But living with Gabby, Rosalinda, and Rosalinda's two other kids—José, age eleven, and Silvia, three—provided, at first, the feeling of an actual home. Sometimes Rosalinda cooked for them. Wilber bought a television and hooked it up to the building's cable.

The twins had their own bedroom again. It was small and dark; their windows leaked, and the carpet was moldy. It was still nicer than their soot-stained room back home. It had a door. They still feared being reported to *la migra*, so to prevent their neighbors or anyone from seeing in, the boys tacked up large fleece blankets in the window wells.

They'd come to adore Gabby's Chihuahua, Nicky. Each

evening they'd coax her into their room. Raúl chuckled as he flipped her over and rubbed her belly. When they finally went to sleep, Ernesto would tuck the dog beneath his chin. When Nicky slept with him, he had fewer nightmares.

Eleven-year-old José became the twins' frequent tag-along. He bounced between his grandmother's house, his dad's house, and Wilber's apartment, where he often ended up sleeping in the twins' room, playing video games and watching movies late into the night. José was younger, which took the pressure off the twins to be mature and tough, and his presence made their small world on Hillside feel more like family.

José let the boys check Facebook on his computer. They'd post the occasional photo of themselves and scroll through their old friends' walls. But this always left them feeling adrift and far away.

Plus, they started to get private messages from friends in La Colonia. "You guys look good," one said. "Living the dream in North America, man!" "Hey, can you send a little money? I need to buy some shoes." The requests for money came almost anytime they posted a photo. Even their enemies, the guys who they were sure had ratted them out to Agustín, asked for favors.

They had no money, but felt a twinge of pride that those guys thought they might. Raúl finally unfriended all of them, even the ones who likely hadn't done anything to him. Because who knew, exactly, where people's allegiances were anymore? They tried not to think about it, but harbored a needling fear that someone might come here looking for them.

"Screw them," said Ernesto, unfriending their ex-friends too. He wasn't in charge of much in his life, but he could block a person with a click.

They pulled into the Oakland Unified School District's enrollment office, in a set of trailers behind an old elementary school on Grand Avenue. Wilber had taken yet another day off work.

"How old are you?" the woman behind the counter asked.

"Seventeen," they all replied at once.

"Yes, you can enroll, as long as you're under eighteen." Relief washed over the brothers.

Given their limited language, they were placed at Oakland International High School (OIHS), where I worked. It was about an hour bus ride from where they lived, and it catered specifically to newly arrived, immigrant English-language learners. The school's 370 students came from more than thirty countries. At the time more than 50 percent were Spanish-speaking, from Mexico and Central America.

The first day, they rode the bus to OIHS in silence. The bus ran through the Fruitvale district, past seedy motels, the outdoor fruit stalls of the Vietnamese shops, and shimmering Lake Merritt, then through Chinatown, and headed into downtown Oakland. There the bus route rode up Telegraph Avenue to OIHS.

The twins were all nerves. They were placed in the tenth grade, which according to the school's programming would give them enough time to learn English, earn all their credits, and if they worked hard, graduate in three years. When Wilber filled out the registration paperwork the week before, he had agreed to this plan. He knew he wouldn't be supporting them for three years of leisurely finishing their studies. No way. But he simultaneously wanted the best for them, and for now they would be in school.

To the twins' chagrin, they were assigned to separate classes but were too nervous to argue. Settling into their seats, they felt as though they'd landed on an alien planet. Back home, all their classmates had been familiar. They knew where Ernesto and Raúl lived, who they hung out with, even who their grandfather was. Here, the twins didn't know a single face, and they couldn't communicate with half the students.

Ernesto made his first friend quickly enough: a kid named Diego, from Mexico. He'd been in the United States a few years and spoke English already, which mixed in with his Mexican-slang-riddled Spanish. He was smart, and class was easy for him, so he spent his time cracking jokes and playing on his phone.

The twins learned quickly—where to stand in line for lunch, how to log into their school emails, how to use Rosetta Stone to practice English, the orders and locations of their classes. Every morning they took great care to shower, slick their hair with gel, and don their new American clothes—which, because they had so few, they had to wash frequently at the nearby Laundromat.

They felt dumb in school for not understanding English, but not the dumbest—it helped that everyone was learning alongside them. If they came to school and tried hard, the teachers promised, they could pass their classes. They'd learn English eventually, and the more they practiced, the better they'd do. In 2014, the year the twins enrolled in school, nearly a third of all students in Oakland were English-language learners.

Oakland International High School had opened in August 2007 as part of a network of public schools designed for newly arrived immigrant students. Each subject was simultaneously a language class, so that students could study standard high school subjects while also acquiring the language skills needed to understand what they were learning. Grades at OIHS were based on a combination of skill, effort, and growth in English, and students were allowed to continue enrollment until the age of twenty-one.

Many students had gone to school for only a couple of years before starting with us; a few had never attended school in their lives. A small minority arrived at OIHS with strong educational backgrounds. The student body was astoundingly diverse in terms of language backgrounds, cultural mores, and life experiences.

Like other schools for immigrants, Oakland International was a mirror of migration from around the world. The first ever class was filled with students from Mexico, China, and Karen State in Burma (Myanmar) (by way of refugee camps in Thailand). Within a few years, as environmental and political crises deepened in Yemen, dozens of Yemeni students enrolled, followed by dozens of Nepali refugees who had been ethnically cleansed from Bhutan. A decade after the US invasions, students from Iraq and Afghanistan joined our student body. And starting in 2013, unaccompanied minors began to fill our seats.

We didn't ask for students' immigration status as per US law, but they and their families often confided in us as they sought support.

Most undocumented kids were unknown to immigration authorities. Unaccompanied minors, however, had been caught—meaning they were in more immediate danger of deportation. There was a strange hierarchy among students: those who had immigration cases were more quickly supported, due to their imminent court date; those who had not been caught, or who arrived with parents, received less support. It was difficult and unfair.

The twins were expected to talk to their classmates, in whatever mishmash of languages they could, to finish their assignments. The more students worked together on projects, the more they had to practice English. (The best way for students to learn English, we saw over the years, was for them to date someone from another country. Love is motivating.)

They met other kids from El Salvador as well as from countries they'd never heard of: Burma, Vietnam, Yemen. Everyone had a story, but most avoided discussing the particulars. Ernesto and Raúl didn't want to out themselves as kids without papers, or kids who had problems with gangsters back home, although unknown to them, others felt that way, too. They kept their mouths shut about the fact that, within a few weeks, they might very well be ordered deported, and they returned home as soon as the bell rang. Walking from the bus stop in the dark made them nervous, and sometimes, as they fell asleep, they thought they heard gunshots—or maybe just a backfiring car.

The night before their court date, Ernesto and Raúl sat up worried. What would they say to the judge? What if he deported them right then and there? What if he accused them of being gangsters? They planned what they would wear—the dark jeans and light blue plaid shirts Wilber had bought them, buttoned up all the way. They checked and rechecked the papers in their manila envelope: their exit paperwork from the shelter, their birth certificates, their Notice to Appear. The judge might ask about their grades, how they liked school, and why they'd left home; they practiced their answers. They would do their best to look like reliable young men.

So focused were they on how to prepare, it never occurred to them to worry about how to find the courthouse.

CHAPTER 9

On a cold, clear day in February 2014, Mr. David, a math teacher, poked his head into my office.

"We have a problem," he said, motioning to two students who stood behind him. Their heads were hung, and their fists gripped around their backpack straps. Despite the brisk weather, the boys sported only black T-shirts and slim-fit blue jeans, and red-and-black Nikes.

"Come on in, gentlemen," Mr. David said, urging them into the stuffy shoebox of an office. The boys reluctantly obliged.

"These two missed their court date," he said. He repeated it in Spanish. The two boys nodded, and suddenly I noticed that their faces were identical. *Twins*.

They introduced themselves: Ernesto and Raúl Flores from La Colonia, El Salvador, they proclaimed somberly.

"Don't worry," I said in Spanish, though they had every reason to.

The twins stood in my office like living statues of fear: fixed eyes, sharp cheekbones, strained expressions. While Raúl laughed nervously from time to time as we spoke about their situation, Ernesto's jaw remained clenched, his gaze severe.

In all probability, after missing court that day, they had been ordered deported. It wasn't likely that immigration authorities would come looking for them, given limited staffing and the fact that kids like the Flores brothers would be low on the priority list. Still, it wasn't uncommon for people to be swept up in immigration raids or to be taken into custody by agents looking for someone else.

Though Oakland was a "sanctuary city"—a loose term meaning that its police force did not hand over people they arrested to the immigration authorities (this was not an explicit law, though, and there were numerous cases in Oakland and elsewhere in which contact with law enforcement had led to deportation). If the twins were picked up for anything that teenagers who happen to be documented *also* freely do—smoking cigarettes in the park during school hours, jaywalking, trying to buy booze—it was not out of the realm of possibility that they would end up in the hands of the immigration authorities.

"Why did you leave El Salvador?" I asked.

They shook their heads. "*Problemas,*" said Ernesto. He paused, then: "We can't go back."

Raúl shook his head again. "No," he said. "We can't go back." They needed a lawyer, and fast.

. . .

In many US court cases, a lawyer will be appointed to a defendant who cannot otherwise afford to pay legal fees. Not so in immigration court. The Floreses would have to either find a pro bono option, or pay. Of course, they had no money—less than none, considering their debt. And they were already asking so much of Wilber. Plus, they'd been cautioned about fake attorneys, often called *notarios*, who promised help with immigration cases, then disappeared with their clients' money.

Though immigrants could apply for protective status, the process was complicated and rarely successful. According to the advocacy group Kids in Need of Defense (KIND), a child without a lawyer was five times more likely to be deported. Judges had no responsibility to treat the case of children without lawyers differently: either the child won immigration relief through the official process and paperwork, or he or she did not.

Very few nonprofits in the Bay Area were taking on these cases, and those that were, were too bogged down to take on new cases. That winter I had called legal agency after legal agency, leaving messages that were never returned, and poring over websites in hopes of finding a pro bono lawyer.

The Flores twins, with their identical faces of fear, were now at the top of my growing list of students in need. I was worried about them. I wrote friends who were attorneys and immigration experts for help.

At the time only one local organization, San Francisco–based Legal Services for Children (LSC), specialized in supporting unaccompanied minors. Besides legal representation, it also provided social work support, counseling, and case management. Due to capacity, its caseload was limited.

A few weeks before I met the twins, I'd begun bringing students weekly to LSC's drop-in hours. The students would anxiously wait in line, and then a paralegal would discuss the details of their case to see if LSC would be able to represent them. Bringing the Flores twins seemed to be worth a try—the only immediate option we had.

A week after we met, we boarded a BART train for San Francisco, hoping for a miracle. I could see they were nervous as the train sloped down into tunnels and screamed against the rails. They clutched their backpacks until we slid to a stop at the station.

The Legal Services for Children office was packed with immigrants, old and young—there was no place to sit but on the floor. It's a high-stakes venue, the pro bono waiting room, and the twins could feel a familiar energy of hope and anxiety in the air. They waited for their names to be called, then disappeared into a small room with a paralegal.

After World War II, a time when millions of refugees fled Nazi Europe, the 1951 Refugee Convention was drafted. It defines a refugee as someone who has fled his or her country owing to persecution based on race, religion, nationality, political opinion, or membership in a particular social group. In 1980 the United States incorporated the international definition of a refugee into domestic law. Asylum status is nearly identical to refugee status, but to win asylum in the United States one must apply from *within* US borders.

Poverty, a quest for opportunity, a desire to reunite with family, and a well-founded fear of violence—these are all motivations for kids like the Floreses to emigrate in the present day. By now, El Salvador, Guatemala, and Honduras have become centers of gang activity—and are among the murder capitals of the world. But how to prove that Ernesto and Raúl were highly endangered and feared persecution? Uncle Agustín was after them, as Raúl's experience in Guatemala had proved well enough. But could they demonstrate that this qualified them for asylum? Even if the twins did find an asylum lawyer (LSC didn't take on asylum cases), they didn't necessarily have a good case.

There were other protective statuses they might apply for. As the LSC paralegals explained, unaccompanied minors could qualify for U visas, for people who'd been victims of a violent crime in the United States and were willing to cooperate with the police, or T visas, for people who had been trafficked for labor or sexual exploitation.

Neither applied to the twins. A more common option was Special Immigrant Juvenile Status (SIJS), which provides protection to immigrant minors who have been abused, abandoned, or neglected by parents. But that wasn't why the twins had decided to leave home.

As they listened to the paralegal, the twins were overwhelmed; it was hard to keep track of their options. But they grasped one thing clearly, which was perhaps worst of all: if they did apply for asylum, they would have to do so separately.

"You probably have a better asylum case than a Special Immigrant Juvenile case," the paralegal told Ernesto. The catch was that Raúl didn't have much of a case at all.

Ernesto balked. He shook his head. "But . . . ," he said, trailing off.

They had the same problem and the same face—shouldn't they have the same fate? But Ernesto had been targeted for violence directly, whereas Raúl was at risk only because he looked like his brother. Ernesto might win; Raúl likely wouldn't.

Ernesto felt terrible. It was his fault that he'd had to leave in the first place.

Regardless, the paralegal told them that they'd review their case and be in touch.

Raúl and Ernesto walked out of the office toward the BART station. Without talking, they boarded the escalator and took the train by themselves. What was there to say?

At home, they got on the old, chugging computer they'd got for free from a local nonprofit and opened Facebook. Raúl had convinced his brother that they needed to make new profiles that were private so they could pick and choose their friends. They added only a few people from their old accounts, then set to work friending their new classmates.

Ernesto posted a mirror selfie of the two of them flexing their pecs, then another of them back in San Jose in their new clothes, still skinny from the desert and the terrible shelter food. Raúl reposted them on his own profile. One day he'd post photos of himself in a suit, or driving a car, to show off what he'd become once he became it.

They'd been in the Hillside apartment for a few months. Seven people—the twins, Wilber, Gabby, Rosalinda, and Rosalinda's two younger kids—were sharing too small a space. Rosalinda resented the kids' messiness, while the boys fought with Gabby over shower time. Increasingly the boys holed up in their own room. No more family meals.

The twins hardly saw Wilber, whose three-hour commute wore on him, as did the long hours under the sun shoveling dirt and trimming hedges. Mostly he hung out with Gabby and drove her to class. He almost never drove the twins anywhere, they noted.

Tensions grew in the apartment. Ernesto blamed Wilber for missing their court date. He felt Wilber didn't understand how bad it had gotten back home, now that he was focused on his life in California. When Wilber made a joke at his expense, or even asked him to take out the trash, he stormed out. "Ernesto!" Raúl pleaded each time Ernesto picked a fight. Wilber was doing his best, if you asked Raúl. "Calm down." Getting mad at the one person they had would just make matters worse.

A fight with Wilber always ended with a fight between the twins. Raúl would retreat into himself, quiet for the rest of the evening. Ernesto would sleep with Nicky cuddled under his arm.

As the days of waiting to hear from the lawyers wore on, their Facebook posts took a turn toward the dark side.

Shit me.

Raúl posted this in English next to three wailing emojis. Alongside an emoji of a gun and a knife, Ernesto wrote:

Fuck this life.

The next week, Ernesto was sent to my office with a note.

"Ernesto keeps motioning to his head with his fingers like a gun, saying he wants to kill himself," it read.

He wouldn't talk. "I'm not going to tell you what's wrong," he said. "So don't try."

"Is it the court case?" I asked. Things at home? Something in El Salvador?

"Everything," he said. "But something else, too. But I'm not going to talk about it." He told me only that it was eating at him, infecting his sleep and now his waking hours, too. He said he'd been having flashbacks more and more often, sometimes in the middle of class.

"It's like a dream, but I'm not sleeping. I haven't told anyone about it," he said. Except his old counselor from the shelter, he added. "Not even Raúl knows."

He promised he wouldn't do anything to harm himself that night and, as is standard practice in many schools, signed a "safety contract." He swore he felt a little better. But he refused to see another counselor about any of this.

"Are you sure?" I said. "I think it would be really good for you to have someone to talk to."

But he wasn't interested in opening up again. "Can I go back to class?" he asked, his gaze already drifting from the room.

CHAPTER 10

Back in La Colonia, things seemed to have calmed down with Uncle Agustín, but Maricela went out of her way to avoid him and her cousins in town. Meanwhile, Ricardo and the younger boys worked in the fields.

Maricela and Ricardo had not been on speaking terms since her pregnancy, as he still blamed her for bringing another problem into their house. It was a stupid feud, anyway, if you asked her; Lupita was now almost two, and it was Ricardo, after all, who'd brought Sebastian around.

These days Ricardo spent more time out of the house, and he would come home reeking of booze, which caused her parents to fret. Maricela worried he would join a gang—or maybe he'd joined one already? She heard he was running with shady guys. Maybe he was just protecting himself by staying on good terms with the gangsters, but it seemed foolish to mess around with any of it.

Maricela's little sisters—Marina, twelve, and Lucia, fourteen—were good kids and took loving care of Lupita, but Maricela couldn't talk to them about real stuff. The siblings she'd been the closest to in age and in temperament—Wilber, Raúl, and Ernesto—were gone.

Not to mention Lupita's father and, in the past couple of years, most of her friends. They had all left for the United States. *Everyone leaves,* she thought. *Everyone.* And here she was, stuck with the twins' debt, with the baby, and with her aging parents. Only twenty years old and already trapped.

She missed going to school. Her whole world was now in the house: all she did was help her mom with chores and take care of her daughter.

One afternoon Maricela turned on a popular matchmaking TV program. People sent messages along with their phone numbers to be displayed at the bottom of the screen, like a live OkCupid or Tinder.

That's how she met Cesar. He was twenty-five and lived in a town on the outskirts of San Salvador, where he worked in a factory. After a few days they switched from Facebook messaging to talking on the phone. The first time she heard his voice, her heart sprung into her throat. He sounded like a really, truly good man.

They got to know each other—what they liked and disliked, what they wanted for their futures, their longings and disappointments and betrayals. He began to say he wanted to be with her. He felt like he could be in love with her and would take her daughter as his own.

The messages thrilled her. For two months she woke up

111

each morning and looked at her phone, planning her day around when she could talk to Cesar. Someone right here in El Salvador who wanted to be with her, someone not so far away.

Due to capacity issues Legal Services for Children declined to take on the Flores brothers' case. The paralegal recommended we call Amy Allen, a private attorney. I left her a message. When my phone rang later that day, Ernesto was sitting in my office. He had gotten in trouble for throwing pens across the room in history class. He said he wasn't thinking of harming himself anymore. When he felt upset, he said, it helped to let it out by throwing things.

I answered my phone, then covered the receiver. "It's the lawyer!" I whispered. Ernesto tapped his foot anxiously.

Amy Allen's tone was cheerful yet professional. She took only SIJS cases, not asylum cases, but said she'd be happy to talk to the twins. Unfortunately, she explained, she didn't work pro bono. The price she quoted was likely impossible, though it was a fraction of what most attorneys charged. I told her I'd talk it over with the boys, and we hung up.

"She can probably take your case," I explained, after Raúl joined us in my office, "but it would cost twelve hundred dollars—each." They looked at each other, then away. Raúl dropped his head between his legs and began rocking from side to side.

"Twenty-four hundred dollars is a lot," Ernesto said, with a grim laugh, "but nothing like what we owe at home." What was another shovelful of money heaped onto the pile of debt?

Amy agreed to accept a payment plan. She'd accept two hundred dollars a month from them, so they could pay off the debt over the course of a year.

They were afraid to ask Wilber. They knew he was struggling to support just their most basic needs. And they'd already asked him for so much.

As Rosalinda prepared dinner that night, she saw that they were discussing something serious and asked what was wrong. Reluctantly they told her their situation. They could get a job to pay for the lawyer, they said, but then they'd have to quit school—yet Wilber had promised the government to get them into school, and dropping out would look bad to the judge. Plus, how would they make a good life for themselves without English, without an education? And they were starting to like school, where, for the first time in their lives, they weren't bullied.

Rosalinda looked at the boys: so young, with a mom so far away. She was silent for a bit, then said, "I can help you for a couple of months."

Raúl shook his head in awe but said nothing.

"We'll pay you back," Ernesto said. "We'll pay everything back."

"Don't worry about that now," Rosalinda said.

A few nights later Gabby told Wilber about the agreement. "Isn't that sweet?" she said.

Wilber's face flushed. The twins had asked Rosalinda? He didn't want to look like a deadbeat to Gabby's family, whom he was still only getting to know. As it was he had enough of a complex about not having papers and speaking so little English.

He stormed into the twins' room. "Rosalinda is not helping you with your lawyer," he said. "I am in charge—you ask me."

"We have to get help from wherever we can," Ernesto spat back. Wilber was treating them like beggars.

"Seriously? Look at all this!" said Wilber, pointing around the disheveled boy den, with soda cans and crumpled clothes everywhere. The beds, the TV, the clothes, the entire bedroom—he paid for all of it.

Raúl sat on the edge of his bed, silent.

Wilber slammed the door, and they heard the car pull out of the driveway. Ernesto punched the mattress hard, and Raúl closed his eyes and dropped his head into his hands. Raúl called Nicky into the room, knowing she would help Ernesto calm down.

The next day Wilber agreed to help them with the lawyer fees, at least for now. He told them they'd have to get jobs, which was fine with them. They'd have to put off sending money to El Salvador a little longer. They didn't tell their parents or Maricela about the new debt they were about to incur.

Cesar lived an hour and a half by bus from La Colonia. He told Maricela to meet him outside the cathedral in his hometown, outside of San Salvador. He'd be wearing a brown shirt, he texted. "You'll recognize me from my photos."

It took three buses to get from her house to his town.

She saw him there waiting for her. He looked just like his pictures—broad chested, a smooth complexion, kind eyes—and even better, because here he was in real life. They hugged politely, which sent electricity down her spine, and he led her to a café. She twirled a spoon into her cup, keeping her eyes on the plastic floral tablecloth. She wanted simultaneously to glow and to vanish.

"It's really good to see you in person," he said. She smiled.

After coffee, he said, "Come to my house. I want you to meet my parents."

The hopscotch of her heart. *Meet his family?* "Okay," she said. As they walked to his house, she relaxed a bit. She could count the number of times she'd sat down at a restaurant on one hand, but visiting a home was something she knew how to do.

After a long and blissful afternoon on the couch sitting as near as she could to Cesar without touching him, she headed home.

When he walked her to the bus, he pulled her into a side street and kissed her. She fell asleep that night imagining their life together. She would move out of La Colonia and have a place of her own.

Attorney Amy Allen rented a space in the Women's Building in the Mission district of San Francisco, a rapidly gentrifying area of the city that was once primarily Latino.

The twins and I left school early on a Friday afternoon

to make their first appointment. Walking into the lobby, we spotted Amy. She was in her early thirties, and her affectionate smile instantly put the boys at ease.

"You must be Ernesto and Raúl!" she said. *"¡Buenas tardes!"* She shook their hands and led them upstairs to her office. Separately and then together, she asked Raúl and Ernesto about everything they'd been through. They talked about their home in El Salvador, about the time they stole corn for the bike and got beaten for it, about their siblings, their school, what happened to Raúl on the way north from Guatemala. Ernesto was quiet about his own trip north.

"I felt sick when I heard what had happened to him," Ernesto said. He started to tear up. "It was my fault." She offered a box of tissues.

"How do you like the United States?" she asked them.

"It's safe here," Ernesto said, "but I miss my family."

"It's better here," Raúl said. Sometimes, they admitted, they still worried that someone from El Salvador could come and track them down. It was unlikely, but it kept them up some nights.

After more than an hour and a half of interviews, Amy shared her thoughts. They could qualify for Special Immigrant Juvenile Status, but didn't have the strongest case. What their uncle and cousins had done to them was terrible, and they could still be in danger, she agreed, but SIJS was for minors who had been abused, abandoned, or neglected by their parents. Wilber Sr. had beaten them growing up, and the family had been unable to protect them from the danger of their uncle, both of which could be deemed qualifying factors for an SIJS visa. She didn't think their case was impossible, "but there would be no guarantees."

Now they just had to go ahead and decide whether or not to apply for SIJS. "Talk to your brother and take some time to think it over," she said. She promised to call them next week.

By that time the fog had rolled in, and they crossed their arms to keep from shivering as they left the building. I had had to leave for another appointment, so they would once again take the BART home, a prospect that no longer frightened them. The long escalator sucked them back underground.

For a judge to order that it is in a child's best interest to stay in the United States, there needs to be a guardian to care for the child. If the twins decided to hire Amy, they'd need Wilber to sign on as their court-appointed guardian. They'd also have to get paperwork, signed by their parents in El Salvador and sent back to Oakland, in which they agreed to relinquish their guardianship. Also, Amy had explained, if they won SIJ status, they could never apply for their parents to join them in the United States. This attempt to win immigration status would mean committing to separation from their family. And all this would have to be decided against the ticking clock of their eighteenth birthday, less than two months away.

Wilber was the decider, and he asked for my advice. I went to his and the boys' apartment, and we sat in lawn chairs outside to discuss. We reviewed the conundrum: the twins had a trusted, low-fee lawyer now, but getting SIJ status was a long shot. On the other hand, they could apply for asylum, but we hadn't found any lawyer willing to take their case for free. And if we missed their eighteenth birthday, the first option—SIJS—would be off the table.

"What do *you* think?" he asked.

I had to admit I really didn't know.

"I can help with the lawyer's fees and they can pay me back," he said.

I reminded him that there was no guarantee they'd win.

He nodded. "But it seems like the only chance, right?" he said.

We sat for a while in the quiet. I told him I admired how hard he was trying to support the boys.

"I worry about them," he said.

"Me too," I said. "Especially Ernesto."

"Yeah," he said. "He has bad dreams sometimes. He wakes the whole house up with his screaming." He paused. "The desert—it's bad."

"Have you talked to them about what happened?"

"A little," he said. "But I know how it is. They'll just cry—and I really hate to see them cry."

I had another question for Wilber, one that had been nagging at me since the twins first told me about why they'd left El Salvador. "The boys said they had to leave because their uncle wanted to kill them. Is that really true?" It seemed outlandish to me.

"Yeah," he said in English. "That's what happened."

"And the tree? He was that mad over a tree?"

"The thing is," he said, "that's how it is in El Salvador." He picked up a pebble. "There, they'll kill you just for doing this"—and by way of demonstration, he pitched the pebble across the lot. We watched it rattle over the other rocks and come to a stop, lost among the rest.

"That's how it is in El Salvador," he repeated. "And that's why they're here."

I thanked him and said good night, then poked my head inside the door to tell the twins I'd see them in the morning.

They shot up out of their seats. "We'll walk you to the car," Raúl offered.

"What did Wilber say?" they asked when we were out of earshot of the house. A homeless man sidled by us, pushing a squeaking shopping cart down the empty street.

"He said it was worth a try."

CHAPTER 11

Wilber read through the responsibilities of a court-appointed guardian. "You are responsible for providing food, clothing, shelter, education, and all the medical and dental needs of the child," the paperwork read. He was already more or less doing these things. "You must provide for the safety, protection, and physical and emotional growth of the child." Wilber wondered if it would be in his best interest to go ahead with this. He had no papers, after all, and here he was, placing himself on the government's radar.

How could he be sure his younger brothers didn't screw up? If they did, would *he* be punished or risk deportation himself? Already they were going to school late or skipping while he worked long hours and shuttled back and forth in the car.

To have a shot at SIJ status, they had to move fast. First

they'd have to file a petition in probate court arguing that going back to El Salvador was against their best interests as children—and since they were technically children only until they turned eighteen in mid-April, they'd need to file a special motion to get a court date immediately. The judge would have full discretion on whether to grant the motion. If he or she didn't, they'd be eighteen, and therefore ineligible, by the time their appointment did come around. Given the time crunch, the judge would be deciding whether to grant the guardianship and the SIJ status on the same day.

If the probate court judge determined that the Flores twins had experienced abuse, abandonment, or neglect, they would issue something called a "predicate order" for SIJS, and Amy would then file an SIJS application with US Citizenship and Immigration Services (USCIS). Once the predicate order was granted, the twins could apply to become legal permanent residents—in other words, get their green cards.

But without Wilber, none of this would be possible.

Wilber spoke to Amy over the phone. Yes, she explained, his name would be entered into official government records, but the courts had no established procedure for handing over his information to immigration officials. And his guardianship would last only until they turned eighteen.

He'd gotten them this far. He signed the paperwork.

Still, the twins wondered whether he would actually go through with being their guardian. Until he showed up at court with them—a legal necessity—there were no guarantees.

Wilber and Ernesto were fighting more than ever. It rattled Raúl. "He's taking care of us," he said to Ernesto. "Give him a break."

"Taking care of who? He doesn't give a shit about us," Ernesto said. "He wished we never came."

Amy, meanwhile, who was working day and night to prep their case, managed to secure them a court date on April 8, three days before their birthday. This was great news—but there'd be no time to appeal their case with a higher court to reverse the decision if they were turned down.

Wilber signed the papers three weeks before April 8. To complete the transfer of guardianship, their parents also had to sign off. How would they get the papers to La Colonia? Their parents had no computer, and mail could take weeks. Emailing the paperwork would be faster, but the document would be less official because it would be hard to prove its origin. A fax would carry a marker of the date, time, and phone number from which the fax was sent, which would prove, at least, that the document originated in El Salvador. Amy suggested emailing the paperwork to Maricela, who would print it at a copy shop, bring it to her parents to sign, and then fax it back to Amy from the shop.

La Colonia's one fax machine was on the fritz, with no prospect of being fixed soon. Maricela offered to go to a neighboring town, a thirty-minute bus ride away.

"I don't want her to go," Ernesto said. He knew bus travel in the area had become dangerous; even performing the short errand was risky. But April 8 was fast approaching.

Things were indeed getting worse around La Colonia. The nearby town had some of the highest murder and disappearance rates in the country. The gangs' ground troops—mostly poor local kids—tracked the movements of daily life. Little things like going to the bank or boarding a bus could put a target on your back. As a resident, to deviate from routine was to put yourself at potential risk.

Maricela knew that the sooner her brothers got papers, the sooner they could start paying back the debt. And in truth, she always relished the opportunity to leave La Colonia. She was going to find a fax machine, she told Ernesto over Facebook.

She hitched a ride to the end of the road that led to the town, Lupita in tow. Lupita was almost two and becoming serious, like Ernesto, with brows that were perpetually furrowed. Despite living in a small, packed house, she was shy around almost anyone besides her mom. Whenever Maricela left to spend the day with Cesar, Lupita wept. She adored her daughter, but didn't she, too, need a life apart?

Now they rode a bus to the neighboring town without incident. Once there, Maricela hoisted Lupita onto her hip, marched through the bustle to the copy shop, and faxed the paperwork to her brothers.

On the ride back to La Colonia, she was triumphant. She'd done something useful, and they owed her now.

Along the main road, three men boarded and walked toward the back, where they drew knives from their pockets. The bus driver either didn't notice or didn't care, and drove on. "Excuse us," they said, flaunting their weapons. They walked the aisles. The passengers knew what to do—heads down, they offered up dollar bills, phones. Maricela knew that as long as she handed something over, nothing was likely to go wrong. She held out a few dollars and her cell phone—the one phone the family had.

The guy attending her aisle grabbed the money and the phone and noticed the gleam of her daughter's gold bracelet, a gift from Lupita's father in the United States. The guy looped his finger under the bracelet and yanked. It broke against Lupita's wrist, and she began screaming. Maricela held her close, trying to lull her to quiet. The thieves got off the bus, and the driver shifted it into gear. They chugged up the road as if nothing had happened.

"I knew she shouldn't have gone," said Ernesto when he heard from Maricela on Facebook. "I knew something would happen." Once again, someone he cared about had suffered on account of him.

But they had the fax. They were ready to go to court.

As in El Salvador, Ernesto fell into socializing easily, and when he was around other people, his panic attacks stayed at bay. Most of the boys' friends at school were also unaccompanied minors. Alfredo, from Guatemala, was big and muscly, with slicked-back hair, a cowboy belt, and silver rings on his fingers. He and his cousin Brenda had been nabbed by *la migra* in Texas.

Sometimes Alfredo's mom would make them food, and they'd play video games or watch Spanish movies, or they'd go watch soccer games at their friend Douglas's house in

Fruitvale. When they could get ahold of it, which wasn't often, they'd pass around a bottle of alcohol.

Ernesto controlled the cell phone, making plans that Raúl was free to join or not. Raúl went along cautiously. His new classmates seemed to be good people, but you never could tell.

At the apartment, when his friends weren't around, Ernesto's bad dreams continued to bleed into his waking hours. Raúl could sense when an attack was coming. They were something between a seizure, a trance, and a fit of rage. Suddenly his brother would seem possessed by a demon. Raúl thought of the corpse in the desert; touch a dead person, he knew, and you could be fouled by their spirit.

"You okay?" Raúl asked from time to time.

"Leave me alone," Ernesto would reply. Or "Mind your own business."

What, really, was going on? There was still something Ernesto wasn't telling him.

Ernesto secured himself a girlfriend from another school, named Marie. They met at a park near Hillside where he and Raúl sometimes went to smoke. She was only fifteen, with long, straight hair. Like Gabby's, Marie's family was Salvadoran, but she was born in the United States, which made her a US citizen. She spoke perfect English and Spanish, which impressed Ernesto. He and Raúl still struggled with English, defaulting to Spanish and afraid to speak up at all in class lest they make any mistakes.

Ernesto talked and texted with Marie late into the night, and in just over a week he used up all their phone minutes for the month. So for the rest of March they could only text, meaning they couldn't accept calls from Amy. Raúl scolded him, but for Ernesto, it had been worth it.

Marie introduced him to her family and to the nicely decorated living room in their home a few blocks away. She and Ernesto would sit and watch TV with her parents, who would serve him sodas and chat with him about El Salvador, about school, like a real family. Ernesto loved it over there. But nothing beat their afternoons at Arroyo Viejo Park, when they could fool around in peace.

"Does Marie know about your court case?" I asked Ernesto.

"No," he said. "No way. I don't want to bother her with all that."

Raúl feigned indifference to his brother's activities. "Who needs a girlfriend? They take up too much time."

"Jealous," Ernesto said.

"No, seriously," Raúl said, "I don't even care."

It was April 8, three days before the twins' birthday—their day in court. I suggested we meet up with Wilber and drive together from the school. This time, we found the courthouse with time to spare.

On the second floor of the courthouse, Amy briefed them again on what was going to happen. When the judge called their names, they would walk to the front of the courtroom. The judge would ask them questions. Amy didn't expect the questions to be hard or complicated, but the boys should know that there was no wrong answer, that they only had to tell the truth. They laughed nervously, their eyes alternating between her face and the floor.

They waited in the pews while several other family cases played out. When the Flores case was called, the boys looked at each other, then at Amy, and stood, adjusting their shirts. We pushed through the low swinging gates and took our seats at the table in front of the judge. Ernesto and Raúl sat like soldiers at attention.

The judge confirmed who was there, then smiled down at the boys.

"I'm granting the guardianship to Mr. Wilber Flores," she said. "And I've read over the petition, and I'm going to approve that, too."

"Thank you, Your Honor," Amy said. She looked at us, smiled, and nodded toward the exit.

That was it?

The Flores brothers walked back down the aisle between the pews of waiting children—first Raúl, then Ernesto, then Wilber. Once out in the bright hallway, they turned and looked pleadingly at Amy, not sure what they had heard.

She broke into a smile. "This is great!" she said. "She granted it!" Meaning both the guardianship and the order establishing their eligibility for SIJ status. The judge had given no verbal explanation—but she'd deemed, based on the twins' written testimonies, that it was in their best interest to be allowed to stay in the United States.

Raúl started laughing. Ernesto's eyes shone with almost-tears. The twins looked at each other for an extended moment. The group exchanged celebratory hugs.

"Wow," said Wilber. "Wow. So lucky. So great."

"Now," Amy reminded us, "immigration still has to approve this, and you'll have to do another interview, but this is a really good sign. They rarely go against what this court recommends." For today they'd had a victory.

The afternoon was bright and warm as the brothers walked to the car, past Berkeley's lush fruit trees.

On the way back to school, the boys watched Berkeley turn into Oakland, and the red lights shift to green, as families of all colors walked across streets, bicycles rattled by, and homeless people wheeled their carts beneath the California sun.

Back at school, still in shock, they ambled across the courtyard, returning to class.

That night Wilber entered the twins' room and sat down on the edge of their bed. "I'm happy for you guys," he said. "I really am. But it's been so easy for you." They'd been here only a short time and had already gotten their papers. "I've been here for seven years." He knew it didn't work that way—papers falling from the sky once you'd been here long enough—but still, he wished.

Ever since the twins had come to live with Wilber, jealousy, that slender snake, had twisted through him on and off—when he dropped them off at school or when he met with their lawyer today in court. He knew the journey had been hard for them, but it was hard for everyone.

For seven years he had commuted to work, scared of being stopped by police, worried that *la migra* would raid his workplace, send him home. For seven years he had felt the everyday racism: a Latino like him could show up in a suit and tie at the nicest restaurant in town and still be treated differently from a grubby white guy in jeans and a T-shirt. Life for an undocumented person was better in Oakland than in lots of other places; in Arizona, for instance, he'd once heard the police stopped Latinos just to check their papers, not even with another pretense, and that their politicians wanted to deport all immigrants. California was better, but still, it wasn't easy. Racism, he knew, was everywhere on Earth but perhaps strongest in the United States, this place home to so many different kinds of people.

There was the way people looked at him when he was one of the only Latino guys in the store, the message of *you don't belong*. Gabby, her family, now his own brothers—they all could legally call this place home. But he still lingered among the eleven million in the shadow zone. Dreams he had—of joining the army perhaps, of getting papers of his own, of feeling respected for just being himself, no matter what his race or background was—were just fantasies.

The twins sat on the bed listening to Wilber. They didn't know what to say, other than they were sorry.

"Don't worry," Ernesto said, in a rare showing of tenderness.

"You'll get papers someday," Raúl said.

"Yeah," Wilber said, "I guess everything comes in its own time."

For the rest of that week, the boys showed up at school on time, did their homework, and took home books to read at night. After nearly a year of struggle, they now saw the potential of life on this side of the border. Even Ernesto slept well.

The twins kept their celebrations between the two of them, out of respect for Wilber and their undocumented friends. They were even shy about telling their teachers they'd taken their first step toward papers. They did tell their parents, and Wilber Sr. and Esperanza knew that the prayers they'd murmured at church had worked.

The twins didn't plan any party for their eighteenth birthday, either. Birthdays back home were never a big to-do; there'd been eleven of them and no extra money. Raúl celebrated by going to a neighboring high school's soccer game, where a friend had arranged for them to meet up with some cute emo girls from another school. He smoked cigarettes, assuming an air of cool. One of them asked him for a cigarette; he felt the thrill of brushing her hand with his, then giving her a light. Nothing came of the outing, but he felt a confidence he hadn't had since he'd left home. He had papers, and he was eighteen—officially a man.

Ernesto, too, spent that first week on a cloud, but the dreams had come back.

Only Raúl was there to shake his twin and sit with him while he calmed his quickened breaths. Eventually Raúl asked his brother point-blank: "Why do you have so many bad dreams?"

For whatever reason Ernesto finally felt like talking. "All right," he said, "I'll tell you."

Raúl perked up, surprised.

"Remember in Reynosa when you went to the bathroom?"

In the safe house, when Raúl had gone upstairs to wash up, Ernesto had sat, avoiding eye contact, on the small mattress they shared on the floor. One of the *coyotes,* the guy who acted like the boss, opened the door. "Help me out back?" he'd said. Ernesto looked up and realized the guy was talking to him.

He followed him to the outdoor area where women were cooking food for the migrants shacked up inside. One of the migrants, who had been complaining about how long he'd been there, was back there, too.

"Why haven't we moved?" he was shouting. "When are we going to get out of this hellhole?"

It was stressful, the waiting—Ernesto had been there only two days, and it had gotten to him, too.

"What am I paying you thousands of dollars for," he continued shouting to the boss, "to just sit here and wait forever?"

The boss slapped him across the face. "We move when I say so, asshole."

Instead of silencing him, the slap turned the man hysterical. He flailed, kicked, and shouted. Ernesto backed up against the cinder-block wall, trying to disappear.

"I've been here for two months!" he cried, spit flying from his mouth. "I paid you people to get me there!"

At this, one of the guides took out a machete and jabbed the long blade into the man's stomach. He fell to the floor, blood pooling out of him.

"Help!" he pleaded, and looked at Ernesto, right in the eyes. "Help me!" But Ernesto was frozen still. He did nothing.

The leader, the one who'd ordered Ernesto back there, took out his gun and shot the dying man in the head. The man's body relaxed into its final slump on the cement. Ernesto fled back inside.

"I saw all this, right in front of me," he told Raúl. He never found out what the *coyote* had wanted from him.

"Why didn't you tell me?" asked Raúl. As far as he knew, it was the first big secret his twin had ever kept from him.

Ernesto hadn't told him back in Reynosa because he couldn't unlock his throat to talk. And also to protect Raúl. To protect them both, really. If Ernesto had blabbed about the murder, what would stop the *coyotes* from offing him, too? After that, Ernesto had tried to push it to the back of his mind.

When he'd fallen on the corpse in the desert the following week—onto some poor, miserable migrant just like them—it was God's way of reminding him: *a man died, and you did nothing, you did nothing, you did nothing.*

That night they stayed up talking and hardly slept. The next morning they arrived late to school.

CHAPTER 12

Ernesto's story was out. After he told Raúl, he told me, then even Wilber, in a flash of intimacy after the court date. But liberating the secret didn't make things any better. In fact, it might have made things worse. To tell what had happened was to give it shape and weight outside his memory.

Alcohol was a balm, and Ernesto started to drink more. The week after he told Raúl about the Reynosa murder, Ernesto was caught drinking at school. A friend had shared a bottle of Gatorade mixed with vodka. Ernesto had guzzled it down. Within the hour he was bleary-eyed and slurring his words in class, then stumbling around the courtyard. He was sent home and suspended for two days.

Ernesto loved that the booze made him feel weightless. The first drink smudged the sharp edges of memory and brightened the world around him as though he'd applied an Instagram filter. Life was nicer-looking through tipsy eyes.

Unfortunately that feeling would wear off. Then the only remedy was sleep, though then he risked bad dreams. He'd wake up the next day feeling heavy and full of remorse yet wanting to chase that lightness again that lifted him off the sad fact of being human, even for a few moments.

"The money?" Maricela wrote to the twins through Facebook. The debt was nearly nineteen thousand dollars now. They didn't write back.

Through friends from OIHS the twins got a job moving boxes. One day a week after school, they'd ride around Oakland picking up parcels and stacking them in a truck. Making money meant they were moving forward.

Their earnings added up to about $640 a month, which they pledged to save and send back to El Salvador. Except just ten dollars for cigarettes—no big deal. And an occasional stop at McDonald's. And they needed new jackets, and their shoes were pulling apart at the seams. All this had to come out of their wages.

By the end of the first month, they had hardly saved any money at all. They'd do better next month, they promised themselves. Ernesto scored another gig cleaning a Japanese restaurant in the ritzy Montclair district once a week. He'd be paid nine dollars per hour. But by the end of the second month, they still only had about $150 to send home—which didn't even pay off the interest accrued *that* month.

The gap between the life they were building in the States and their family's dire situation in El Salvador overwhelmed them. Yet they worked hard, and didn't they need food and shoes?

As a distraction the twins redoubled their efforts to make friends, to inch their way into a cooler crowd while still keeping more innocent friends like Alfredo. They plotted over who could get a hold of booze (more money gone); they made more connections over Facebook; and they sneaked out of class, and even smoked pot a few times on the corners after school. They dropped five dollars on street tacos after work. They got iPhones, a previously unimaginable luxury. They needed them to find their way around Oakland, they reasoned.

At Oakland International, regular classes ended just before Memorial Day. The final three weeks were spent in a single intensive class, with a mixed-grade group of students. I, along with the twins' math teacher, Mr. David, taught a hiking-and-camping class that earned students PE credits. Ernesto was in our group.

We'd take two trips: the first to a local farm; the second, a two-day hike where we'd be backpacking. Ernesto skipped the orientation day, having slept in. He'd been coming to school less and less; when he slept during the day, he seemed to have fewer nightmares. He showed up just as we were getting into the cars to leave on the first trip. He didn't know anyone in our group apart from Diego, his first friend and former tablemate. Ernesto plugged his ears with headphones and faced the window as we crossed the San

Rafael Bridge toward the Marin Headlands before turning onto the golden hills and the wide vista of the Pacific.

We spent the afternoon milking goats and turning compost, walking across the tidal zones in search of starfish and sea cucumbers, watching the sea collide against the craggy edge of the continent. Ernesto stood off to the side, his face a mask of indifference.

A beetle ambled slowly across our paths. Its black armor had an iridescent green sheen, and we bent to inspect it.

"Look how beautiful!" one of the girls said.

"Wow!" another cooed.

Ernesto walked over to the bug and stomped on it. Then he laughed and walked away.

That night at the campfire, the students roasted marshmallows and played I Spy. Ernesto played on his phone. Later, when he crawled into a tent, he smelled smoke. "Cigarettes?" he asked the boys who were lounging in their sleeping bags, listening to music.

"Yeah, man, you want one?" asked Ibrahim, a skinny senior from Iraq who drove a gold rattletrap Mercedes, dressed hip-hop, and smiled often.

"Yeah," Ernesto said. They turned out their lights and walked across the moonlit field to an outcropping out of sight of camp.

Ernesto inhaled deep into his lungs and exhaled into the dark. Newer students generally stuck to friends from their own language group, but older students like Ibrahim, who had learned more English, often branched out. He wanted to learn some Spanish, too, because he had a Mexican girlfriend from another school.

Ernesto thanked him for the smoke. They could hardly see each other in the dark and didn't talk—Ibrahim didn't speak much Spanish yet, and Ernesto still barely spoke English. They just sat in each other's company, watching the waves shatter.

The following week we left for the second trip, which was in Big Basin Redwoods State Park, a thick swath of redwoods that plunged from the Santa Cruz Mountains to the sea. Our bus snaked slowly up the narrow roads to the park entrance while the students whooped and hollered from the back seats. Ernesto, by now, had made multiple friends in the class, including an older Salvadoran girl and two Guatemalan sisters who called him things like "Ernestito" and "my Ernesto."

The first hike was an eight-mile trek that culminated in a steep ascent up a cliff alongside a waterfall. Ernesto didn't complain as we scrambled over rocks and up ladders, and he offered repeatedly to take some of the weight from other students. He carried an extra jug of water on behalf of the group; he took on another cooking pot; and he stuffed extra clothing and water bottles into the spare pockets and corners of his backpack. His face seemed to loosen as he hiked. At one point I turned around to check on the group, and I saw him walking alone in silence, smiling.

At night he and Ibrahim snuck off for a cigarette, along with Diego, who also spoke near-perfect English and so could translate.

"You have a twin brother?" Ibrahim asked.

Ernesto nodded—*twin* was an English word he'd learned early on. Ibrahim had realized this, he explained, when he said hi to a kid who he thought was Ernesto and had been ignored.

"I was like, 'What the hell, man. I'm your friend, Ibrahim!' And you didn't say nothing. And then I figured it out!" Diego translated, and Ernesto laughed.

"That's crazy, man, a twin."

The three smoked in silence for a while, and then Ernesto, in English, asked Ibrahim where he was from.

"Iraq," Ibrahim said.

"Damn," Ernesto said in English. Then in Spanish: "Why are you here?"

Ibrahim explained he'd had to leave Iraq because his dad had worked with the US government. He had a sister, Sara, who was a tenth grader at our school. "One day my sister walked out the door to go to school." The family had drivers, he said, because it wasn't safe for them to drive their own cars. "She got outside, and the driver was screaming at her, 'Go back! Go back!' But she didn't know what to do or what was going on, so she couldn't move. And he pointed, and there was a bomb right there. Right next to her." If she had knocked against the bomb, it would have detonated, killing her and, possibly, the whole family.

"So we had to come here," Ibrahim said. "Refugees."

"Wow," Ernesto said after Diego finished translating,

and shook his head. "Damn." They took long drags from their cigarettes. "I'm sorry." Then after a while: "Me too. I had to come here because they were going to kill me, too."

"Shit, man," Ibrahim said. "See? Arab, Latino, white, black—we're all the same. Same shit, good shit, bad shit—same shit."

They lit up another round of cigarettes.

The second day's hike was far less strenuous, but we were all sore from the day before. Ernesto kept up with Ibrahim and some of the older boys from Yemen. When we got to camp, the students collapsed, barely able to muster the energy to put up their tents and cook dinner.

After camp settled down, a commotion arose.

The Guatemalan sisters, whom Ernesto had befriended, ran out of their tent shouting, spewing curses in Spanish, threatening to beat up another group of girls who were sleeping. Those other girls had played a prank on them, they insisted.

Ernesto sat off to the side, shaking his head and muttering. "They're not going to get away with this!" he suddenly shouted. "The bitches, messing with my friends!" He stood up and stamped over to the sleeping girls' tent. He kicked it, then yanked out one of the poles, ripping a long gash in the tent's side. The girls inside gasped and screamed.

Ernesto backed away. Someone shone a light on him; his eyes were unfocused, and he was swaying on his feet.

I pulled Ernesto aside, and Mr. David went to deal with the girls.

"You've been drinking," I said. "You need to calm down."

"I don't care!" he shouted again. "I don't care about the tent. I'll pay for it, I don't care. Those girls have to pay for what they did to my friends."

His crew had smuggled Four Lokos in his backpack. Today Ernesto had taken one down to the trickling stream, along with one of Ibrahim's cigarettes, and sipped it leisurely. In the past he'd drunk to blur his own edges, but today he was drinking in celebration. Today he was happy with the world as it was.

The problem was, as always, that the celebratory feeling didn't last. Now he sat off to the side, head between his knees. He'd had too much, he said, and didn't feel good.

"Why did you drink?" I asked. He'd been doing so well, I'd thought.

He picked up his head and looked at me, the beam of his headlamp shining into my eyes. "Why do you think?" he spat. "Because! Because! Because of my family!" He dropped his head back to his knees and began sobbing. "Because of everything that happened, everything."

His cries came out dry and deep from his midsection. For twenty minutes he let out yells that became sobs, rocking himself forward and back. He eventually quieted into a state of heavy breathing and slow rocking.

"I could have stopped him," he said. "You know? I could have." Reynosa, he meant, the restless migrant with the bullet in his head crying for help.

"You would have risked your own life," I said. "There was nothing you could do."

"I could have tried." He spoke softly now. "I could have tried to do something."

"Then you'd be dead too."

"Maybe better."

He went to stand up. I helped him to his feet, but he shook me off and turned away.

We sat for more than an hour while he drank water and vomited.

"Sorry about the tent," he said finally. "Sorry, sorry, sorry."

The next day, when Ernesto returned home, Raúl asked, "How was camping?"

"Fine," he replied, then went to sleep without saying anything else.

Raúl, for his part, had been assigned to a day-hiking class. He often missed field trips because he came late to school, and he hadn't made any friends in the class. He wished he'd gotten to sleep outside and spend time in the woods, as he and Ernesto had back home when they were just boys, guarding the animals and chatting beneath the stars.

Meanwhile, they were starting to see on Univision and hear at school about a new flood of immigrants. Kids, mostly, who were unaccompanied minors like them. In May 2014 alone, authorities caught more than nine thousand unaccompanied minors along the southern border. That made about 47,000 since October 2013.

As always the migrants came for a host of reasons, but

141

increasingly their primary motivation was fear of gang violence. Immigrant rights advocates like the Women's Refugee Commission (WRC) and the national organization Kids in Need of Defense claimed that these children were, and should legally be considered, refugees. People coming to the United States from dire situations abroad—from Syrians in Turkey to Eritreans in Ethiopia—were granted refugee status. Why did Central American migrants, on the other hand, continue to have to apply for immigration relief one by one—and hope they qualified?

Ernesto took to leaving the room when the news came on the TV at Hillside. Raúl, though, thought about the crisis more and more. He didn't like how people talked about immigrants like they were some kind of parasite. Sure, they crossed the border without permission, but no one wanted to leave home, their parents, for no good reason.

The more they watched and heard, the more scared the twins felt for their family. The same things that were pushing out all these people were bearing down on them, too.

The US government ran out of shelter beds because of this new surge in child migrants. During the first unaccompanied minor spike in 2012, authorities had been unprepared; now in 2014 they too raced to catch up, shacking children up in former nursing homes and military bases and releasing families from overcrowded, austere detention facilities with a court summons.

Hielera conditions were no longer just for temporary holding stations; they were now, in many places, the detention norm. In June the Federal Emergency Management Agency (FEMA) was called in to help seek potential short-term shelters; their standards were extremely low and betrayed very little care for the people who actually would have to stay *in* the facilities. Showers and toilets were deemed preferable but "not necessary" so long as there was outdoor space for "staging areas for shower/restroom/laundry/kitchen trailers, etc." Their suggestions for potentially workable locations included "office space, warehouse, big box store, shopping mall with interior concourse, event venues, hotel or dorms, aircraft hangers [sic]"—provided that they were vacant and able to be leased. The kids would be housed there until a sponsor like Wilber could be found and was willing to take them in and make sure they got to court.

President Barack Obama called what was happening at the border "an urgent humanitarian situation." He requested billions of dollars in additional funding from Congress, largely for housing and related costs. The original $494 million that the president had allocated for housing in 2013 didn't even come close to footing the year's bill. In July 2014, during the thick of the crisis, the Obama administration authorized $3.7 billion in emergency supplemental funding, $1.8 billion of which was earmarked for nonprofit housing contractors and medical providers. That year Southwest Key received more than $156 million in government grants.

Each year detaining immigrants in the United States costs about two billion taxpayer dollars. More than 60 percent of immigrant detainees are held in facilities managed by private contractors like the GEO Group, which houses between eight and nine thousand adult immigrants at any one time and rakes in $140 million per year since 2012. Contractors often cost less per inmate than government facilities—which means there is little federal oversight, and inmates are mistreated, sometimes even abused, without consequences.

The Mesa Verde ICE Processing Facility, an immigration detention center in Bakersfield, California, is one of many border overflow facilities for adults who have just been apprehended after crossing the border. Mesa Verde's contract with the government guarantees it a minimum of 320 immigrants at any one time (out of its four-hundred-person capacity), for a payment of $119.95 per immigrant per day. The government pays a cut rate of $94.95 per immigrant per day for any inmates above the minimum.

The more detainees who are being held, the more money detention facilities make—and the more corporations, and the politicians who support them, do too.

CHAPTER 13

Maricela was feeling tired and a bit nauseous. But it was impossible; Cesar was sterile after an accident many years ago. She bought a home pregnancy test. Sure enough, she was pregnant.

She wanted to tell Cesar in person. "I'm coming there," she texted. On the bus she rehearsed what she might say. She expected him to be mad, or to disappear as Sebastian had. But when she told him, voice unsteady, he hugged her.

"This is the best news I've ever gotten," he said. He had thought himself unable to make a kid. He already knew she was a good mom to Lupita. He had no job, but he loved her, and he promised he'd be a good dad and husband. They talked about getting a place together.

She prepared to tell her parents. She got the worry and disappointment she'd been expecting, but she hadn't been expecting Ricardo's reaction, far worse than it had been with Lupita. He stormed into her room, screamed at her to get out of the house.

"If you don't leave," he told her, "I'll join a gang to take care of the family." This didn't feel like an empty threat.

Once again she found herself on the run. She went with Lupita to her maternal grandmother's house, but there wasn't space to stay long-term, and anyway, how would she support herself? She could have gone and lived with Cesar's family, but they were fighting a lot. Her parents knew that Ricardo had run her out of the house—and they'd done nothing to stop him. To her it seemed that they were scared of their own son.

When the twins found out about Maricela from Ricardo, Ernesto took to Facebook to scold her. Didn't she know, he wrote, that you had to think about the consequences before you acted? Raúl flopped onto the mattress and sighed. They could hear in Ricardo's messages that he was furious. It seemed like a good thing that Maricela had gone away for a while.

The twins enrolled in summer school to improve their English and get credits from the classes they'd failed that spring—largely from absences. They knew they should go, but the first morning they showed up, they were already sick of being stuck inside the school walls. They spent the rest of the week devising schemes to ditch.

Cutting classes and goofing off got them suspended. The district had a strict policy, and since they'd already missed so much summer school, they weren't allowed to come back. This meant that Raúl and Ernesto missed out on three weeks of coursework that they both needed to graduate and to improve their English.

Over the following weeks, Ernesto saw Marie as much as he could, but she was busy in summer school. He worried she wasn't as interested in him anymore. She took a while to respond to his texts, and sometimes didn't respond at all.

One restless afternoon he took a walk to Arroyo Viejo and lit a cigarette. In the corner of the park he saw a girl with long hair sitting next to a guy. It was hard to be sure, because right as he arrived, the two began making out, but her sleek dark hair had to be Marie's.

Ernesto froze for a moment, then turned around. He stormed home. He immediately blocked her on Facebook and Instagram. "You're a traitor," he texted her. "You don't care about me. Never talk to me again."

All night Raúl got texts and phone calls from Marie. What was wrong with Ernesto? What happened? Why won't your brother talk to me? Raúl didn't know how to answer her. Twin code meant he was on his brother's side.

Ernesto changed his profile picture to a photo he took in the bathroom, sunglasses and hat on, no shirt, flexing his muscles.

The number of unaccompanied minors at Oakland International was increasing. Many had had problems back home and were shackled with debt, and all had bad memories of their trips north. And they all needed lawyers.

In a way seeing all these other kids in his same shoes fortified Ernesto, as when Ibrahim had told him about fleeing Iraq. He and Raúl made a pact to not drink so much that year and to really focus on school: eleventh grade.

And they'd focus on the debt. No amount of cash they managed to send home—one hundred, two hundred, five hundred dollars—made a dent, because the interest was growing faster than they could pay it off. They called home every couple of weeks, and every time their father asked: Did they still need to be going to school for their case? Could they leave and start working? Their mother didn't pressure them so much. "I'm glad you're in school," she said.

"Once we get our papers," Ernesto said each time to his father, "we'll be able to pay it off easy." They called home less and less often.

In order for their SIJ status visa to be approved by the US immigration authorities, the twins had to attend an interview with an immigration official in downtown San Francisco, where they'd be questioned both separately and together. They would be asked simple questions, mostly: what life was like for them with their families, when they left El Salvador, when and how they'd entered the United States, where they lived now, and whether they went to school.

Amy practiced with the boys. "Just answer honestly," she said. "And don't be nervous." But what if they gave answers the interviewer didn't like? And what if they had to talk about what had happened in the desert, or in Reynosa, or in Guatemala, in front of a stranger?

The twins' English class was writing newspaper articles about the border crisis. The day before his SIJS interview, Ernesto turned in his paper:

UNACCOMPANIED MINORS

By Ernesto Flores

Many children are crossing the border for a better life. In 2012 police caught 13,000. And 2013 there were even more 2014. Many young people come to the US without parents. They are leaving from Central America. Many come because the gangs make their life very difficult. Many of them are arrested by the police officer.

The government can less the problem by, helping the children considered, as refugees because in their home country many times. They don't have enough help to protect everyone to the gangs. For this reason I think the government from the US can help them. The president he can make a law to, protect every children who come to the United States without parent. I know in this country we have a lot of opportunities to a better life, for begin a professional, no can think for many reasons how protect immigrants children.

I think the government can work how, they can protect the immigrant children here in the United States. The police officer and the government they can not stop the children to cross the border, every children know that it's dangerous, but they want a better life for them, and for their family.

After a spotty six months of American high school, finishing this assignment and expressing himself in English was a huge accomplishment for Ernesto. The biggest improvement was in his effort.

The next day the boys walked out of the interview in downtown San Francisco with doubts about how it had gone. Amy assured them that they'd done great, but they weren't so sure.

Away from home, Maricela found a job as a maid. She worked until she was about to burst, cooking and mopping, washing and folding the laundry. A little more than a month before her due date, she gave up: it was time to go home. She couldn't stay at her grandmother's house forever, and Ricardo must have cooled off by now, she figured.

The labor of the second child was much easier than the first, and it helped having Cesar at her side. It was another girl. Maria Elena, as they named her, or Leiny, was perfect.

Up north the Flores twins were growing up and settling into an unaccustomed permanence, while their sister was, with this new baby and with Cesar, dropping the anchor into her Salvadoran life. All the elder Flores siblings were setting roots into circumstances they hadn't fully chosen. But the baby offered a wink of optimism, family wide.

"You have another niece," their mom announced proudly the next time the twins phoned. During that call no one mentioned the debt.

• • •

The twins' green card approval notices arrived at the end of September. Amy called me early in the morning—the twins weren't answering their cell phones, so she was hoping to track them down at school. I drove around the neighborhood, hoping to find them, and sure enough, they were two blocks from school smoking cigarettes with furrowed brows. I told them Amy had news.

"We know," Raúl spat, shaking his head. "We already know."

I was confused. "What do you mean?"

"We got the letter," he said, pulling his from his backpack. The approval notices had arrived in the Hillside mailbox last night.

"It's bad, right?" Raúl said.

I looked at them in disbelief. "What? No! It's good news. It's really good news!"

"Don't joke around with us," Raúl said gravely. "Just tell us the truth."

I told them. The twins looked at each other, then back at me.

"Are you sure?" Ernesto snapped.

"Yes," I said. "Your applications were approved!"

They looked at each other again, then smiled. Their smiles became embarrassed laughter. Raúl shook the letter.

The paper looked like any intimidating piece of bureaucracy. They hadn't been able to read it. "We thought it said we'd been rejected."

I looked at the paper. "Why did you think that?"

They shrugged. "Just didn't look like good news."

CHAPTER 14

Ernesto began working five nights a week at the Japanese restaurant in Montclair, and soon thereafter Raúl got a job at an Italian restaurant down the road. Together they'd be making several hundred dollars every week.

They both spent evenings busing tables, and after the customers left, they emptied the trash; scrubbed the sinks, stovetops, and counters; and mopped the floors. They'd take the bus back into the Temescal neighborhood, then wait for the number one bus to take them back east. They walked the ten blocks home guardedly.

Once, while waiting for Raúl outside the corner store near their house, a guy Ernesto had never seen before came up and slugged him full force in the face. He fell down onto the pavement, his vision going dark. Before he could say anything, the guy helped him up.

"Whoa, sorry, man," he said. "I thought you were

someone else." Ernesto's mouth was bleeding, and a hunk of a back molar had broken off. He ran home.

A few weeks later Raúl was taking the bus home one night from work alone, which was rare. As he waited for the bus, a group of six guys, covered in hoods and low-slung skullcaps, ran up to him.

One grabbed him from behind. "Give us your money!" another one shouted.

He froze. It was like he was back in Guatemala, head in the dirt. "Give it to us!"

He couldn't move. They frisked him, grabbed his wallet out of his jeans—it had about fifty dollars—rifled through his backpack, and took his phone. They ran off and left him there in the vacant street where he stood, immobilized, until the bus came.

Oakland was a great city but not without its problems. Over the years dozens of Oakland International students had been jumped or mugged on their way to and from school—a few times even at gunpoint within a few-block radius of OIHS, a much safer neighborhood than where many of the students lived.

Crime happened at all times of day, but the twins were really wary only at night. From the bus stop, they walked briskly together, trying to appear determined, fearless, and simultaneously fearsome, puffing cigarettes with *don't fuck with me* expressions. Inside, their hearts were pounding.

Tensions were building at home, and not just between Ernesto and Wilber. Rosalinda's new boyfriend had moved in with them and had invited two of his friends to rent the fourth room. The already full house now had three more grown men living in it, whom the twins referred to as "the Mexicans." Sober, they were nice enough people, but in the evenings they became rowdy. They guzzled beer and cranked music, their voices growing louder as the night went on.

The twins got used to avoiding the living room. No more watching family movies with the kids stretched out on the living room's couches.

One night they overheard the Mexicans talking shit about them: about Wilber's bad attitude, about the mess the boys made in the kitchen and the bathroom. Another day one of them accused Ernesto and Raúl of eating all his cornflakes. That wasn't their fucking food, he scolded. They had clearly been badly brought up to think they could steal other people's stuff.

The twins insisted they hadn't touched the cornflakes.

"Who did it, then?" he wanted to know.

A few days earlier they'd watched Rosalinda's son, José, scarf down several bowls with milk that also wasn't his. But pointing the finger at the boy felt wrong. They shrugged.

They hung out in their room with Nicky. Ernesto was still heartbroken about Marie, but he didn't talk about it, even with Raúl. He hoped she'd see his photos online and feel jealous.

The Mexicans' presence stressed Wilber. Gabby overheard them accusing Wilber and his brothers again of eating all their food. "I'm gonna beat the shit out of him," one of them slurred, referring to Wilber.

Wilber talked to Rosalinda—this wasn't what he'd bargained for when he opted to move in with Gabby's family. But she shut him down. Did he know what it was like to be a single mom of three kids? What was his problem?

Gabby took her mom's side. "Just ignore them." Much as she could have done without the Mexicans, in her eyes Wilber's attitude just made it worse. The couple fought about it, and about other things, too. Money was one. Wilber needed to push his little brothers to help out more, she said. Wilber didn't disagree, but he didn't like her butting in. The twins could hear them arguing through the walls in low, tense murmurs, then in shouts.

The twins had made accidental enemies like their schoolmates back in La Colonia or these Mexican housemates all their lives. But the cause was more than just the fighting words, the bad looks, the accusations that they thought were directed at them. It was what was beneath them, Ernesto and Raúl felt. Those looks accused the boys of being nothing.

One night a few weeks later, the Mexicans, drinking beer and eating a bucket of chicken with the TV blaring, dropped a plate of bones on the carpet next to Nicky. The Chihuahua spent the rest of the evening chewing at the bones.

The next morning Nicky seemed distressed, trembling more than usual. Gabby and Wilber figured she just had the flu.

That evening when the boys came home from school, they found Gabby in her room hunched over, crying. There was Nicky, splayed out on her little blue dog bed, unmoving. Dead.

A vet took X-rays that showed splinters of bone stuck in her stomach and throat.

"Those fuckers killed her," Ernesto spat.

The next day Wilber and Gabby held a private burial for Nicky. Wilber held Gabby while she shook with sobs. "We have to move," she told him.

The twins agreed. "We're moving," they told me gravely the next day. They'd sooner sleep on the streets than spend another night with those dog killers, they said.

Through Wilber's coworkers at the landscaping company, he, Gabby, Ernesto, and Raúl found another apartment, a two-bedroom in a building closer to downtown Oakland (and closer to school). Gabby bought another dog from the pound, a little white fluffball mutt they named Nicky Two. They were ready to start over. It was February 2015, just more than a year since they'd moved to the Oakland apartment.

The main room of the new apartment was an adjoined kitchen and living room, off of which were the two bedrooms—one for Wilber and Gabby, one for the twins—and a bathroom. The home was newly renovated and let in more light than the apartment on Hillside had. It was also more expensive, so the twins ramped up their hours at the restaurants, working five to six days a week to pay their five-hundred-dollar share of the rent. They also needed to pay off their legal fees. Though Amy never once pressed them for the money, they wanted to keep their promise.

There still wasn't much left over for paying down the debt in El Salvador.

"You need to be sending at least a thousand dollars a month," Maricela told them. They knew she was right; the interest was compounding the debt so much that anything much less than a thousand wouldn't even begin to hack away at the principal.

"It's not as easy as it seems," Ernesto said. She had no idea of all the things they were trying to balance.

From Maricela's perspective, her brothers had it great: jobs, school, freedom from the gangs and from their family—everything she didn't have. Cesar was working and helping to support her, Leiny, and Lupita, which helped, but he still couldn't afford a ring or a wedding; she would have moved in with him anyway, but he felt he didn't have enough stability, and things with his parents were rocky. She waited patiently. She still felt confident, if a bit shakier than before, that they'd be together.

She wasn't so confident when it came to her brothers. She'd seen the pictures they posted online. She knew that Ernesto had bought an iPhone. Beyond the rent and fees, the twins felt they spent relatively little on themselves and that what they did was justified. Raúl needed a new pair of shoes because his were falling apart again. Ernesto needed a jacket—it was cold at night, waiting for the bus after work.

Raúl picked out hundred-dollar Nikes; Ernesto's jacket was Nike, too, costing seventy-five dollars. From what Maricela could see on Facebook, these were massive purchases. Wilber had left promising to help the family; he hadn't done much, but at least he'd paid off the debt. The twins had dug a deep hole for the family and scrambled out themselves. "Ask them," their father pleaded, "to not buy so many clothes."

Maricela thought the threat of losing the land might kill her father. "Why are you still in school?" she wrote to the twins. Surely they could work full-time at least for a while, to make sure they weren't responsible for destroying their family.

The twins didn't want to leave school—they wanted to learn English and graduate. The irony was that the after-hours jobs they had taken, to make school possible, were ruining their grades. The first year they had earned mostly Cs, but now they were almost failing. By four o'clock they had to run out the door for work. They had no time for homework or studying. They got home at eleven p.m. on a good night, but with bus delays and on busier nights at the restaurants, they often weren't home until after midnight. On a good day they woke up around eight a.m.; the school, an hour-long bus ride away, rang its bell at 8:20. And though the new apartment was forty blocks closer to school, the buses were often full by the time they reached the twins' stop and passed them by.

Teachers had suggested they repeat tenth grade, since they'd missed so much school and had only enrolled in February. The suggestion that the twins couldn't hack it was unacceptable to them—they'd nearly graduated high school in El Salvador, after all. Yet now, due to their spotty attendance, they were woefully behind their classmates.

Ernesto could come up with enough answers to complete his homework when he tried, and to appear not lost on the days he showed up to class. But when he saw how far behind he was from most of the other students, he felt they must all think he was stupid. He was used to being the smart one, and now, after nearly a year without Raúl by his side in class, he felt anything but. Raúl, though he had weaker English and fewer academic skills, fared much better. Because he was used to needing extra help from Ernesto, he had no trouble asking teachers questions.

They decided that things would be better if they were in the same class. Ernesto took to walking out of his classroom early on in the period and wandering over to Raúl's classroom, where he'd pull up a chair next to his brother. Teachers would repeatedly ask him to leave, but then noticed that, actually, the Floreses *did* get more work done when they were together.

As the spring semester drew on, things did get better. They weren't entirely failing. People saw what the twins had long felt: they were better as a duo than apart.

Ernesto started work on his final portfolio, a presentation to be made to a group of his peers and teachers at the end of the semester. An early slide was titled "One Struggle." "My struggle was that i am absent in the every day in the school," he wrote in white letters against a blue backdrop. "I try to come every day. I had to work in the afternoon, finished in the night."

He was proud, looking back. Last year he had been a scared boy: drunk, stricken with night terrors and guilt. Now, almost a year and a half after breaking down on the camping trip, he had papers, friends, a job, and an apartment, and he knew his way around Oakland. Okay, he scarcely had time for homework or sleep, and his grades weren't the best. But look at him now—presenting in English in front of the whole class.

When he was in the right frame of mind, he could see that his life had righted itself, somewhat, and in spite of all the challenges, his future was, when the light caught it just right, full of potential again.

These days they barely saw Wilber, returning home late as they did, and they'd wake up after he'd already left for his shift.

Occasionally Wilber planned day trips for the family. The brothers sometimes went with Gabby and her brother, José, to the beach in Half Moon Bay, or for a hike. But Ernesto usually either declined these outings or wasn't invited. Wilber drove Raúl up to the hills one day, just the two of them. They came across a pack of goats and fed them apples. Passersby might not know that these young men in skinny jeans had been skilled farmers and shepherds when they were kids. Raúl filmed the herd munching grass on his new, replacement phone. When Raúl showed Ernesto the video, his twin rolled his eyes.

Though things had gotten better between Ernesto and Wilber once they moved out of the Hillside apartment, after

160

a few months they were back at each other's throats: Ernesto didn't clean up his dishes, Wilber didn't drive him somewhere he'd promised, Ernesto had a bad attitude, and on and on.

After a particularly bad fight, Ernesto exploded, telling his older brother to fuck off, that he didn't need him, that he was leaving. A few days later he heard from friends at work about an available bedroom that would cost five hundred dollars a month, and it was settled. He moved out the next day.

Raúl, as usual, was in the middle. If he left with his twin, he would piss Wilber off, and his big brother would be stuck with a two-bedroom apartment that he and Gabby couldn't afford. "He found this place so we could all live together," Raúl reasoned. But he didn't like the idea of living apart from his twin—or taking on Ernesto's share of the rent.

"Do what you want, doesn't matter to me," Ernesto said as he crammed his stuff into his backpack.

Ernesto's new place was in the three-bedroom lower level of a duplex farther east. He shared it with a middle-aged couple and a single guy in his thirties. He put a lock on his bedroom door and came and went as he pleased. He liked having a place of his own, independent from Raúl—something he'd never had before. He could keep his things organized. Apart from the line in the morning for the shower, it felt like a pretty good place for Ernesto. And anyway, he saw his twin every day at school.

On Tuesdays, their day off from work, Raúl spent the night at Ernesto's. Sometimes on other days, too. They'd stay up late, listening to music on low and texting and falling asleep on the small bed.

When Raúl wasn't at Ernesto's, he hung out with friends during lunch sometimes, and in class, but there wasn't really time after school to socialize. He had more time alone, to think and to remember.

Through a friend at work, he found a girlfriend, who lived in San Jose. He skipped a few days of school that spring to go down and see her, taking the bus from the East Oakland terminal. They understood each other, Raúl felt, and texting her all night, he felt less lonely.

But the twins' girlfriends came and went that year. They found most of them through friends of friends on Facebook, or WhatsApp or Kik, a chatting app. They'd strike up a flirtation, and eventually, if things went well, they'd agree to meet in person. The connections rarely lasted long. They never had the time.

Raúl posted on Facebook in English:

I'm fucking single.

Money was tight, and Wilber, Gabby, and Raúl did not pay their rent on time. After four months living there, they thought they'd get some leeway, but the landlord ordered them evicted: they had two weeks to move.

Once they got the eviction notice, Raúl and Wilber decided to part ways. Temporarily, anyway.

At least now he wouldn't have to choose between Wilber and Ernesto, Raúl thought. The eviction had given him a clean break, a good reason for moving in with his twin.

But suddenly Ernesto didn't seem so sure about welcoming him. "You're too messy," he said the week before move-out day. "My room's too small; there's no space. You'll have to find some place of your own."

"Fine," Raúl said, narrowing his gaze. "Whatever."

Raúl shook the conversation off. Ernesto was just playing around, was all.

But when Ernesto said the same thing later that afternoon, Raúl took it harder. "You think I want to live with your stupid ass?" Raúl said. "Fucking animal."

After the final afternoon bell rang, Raúl sat outside school on the cement retaining wall, waiting for Ernesto. His shoulders were hunched, his head hung over his phone.

Passing by, I stopped and sat down next to him. "How are things?" I asked.

"Fine," he said. I asked if he wasn't worried about the eviction; he didn't answer right away. I told him about short-term shelter options in Oakland, where he could go anytime if we couldn't find him a more permanent place to stay.

"Shelter?" he said. "Like in Texas? No, miss, thank you, but I can't go to a place like that."

Just then Ernesto spotted us and came over.

Raúl bolted up. "Gotta go to work," he said, and walked toward the bus stop.

I asked Ernesto how things were going. "Oh, fine," he said. "Things are good, miss. Remember how bad they were last year? It's not like that anymore. Things are really starting to get good."

163

Was he not worried about his brother, with all the stress of the move?

"No," he said. In his eyes they were getting along great.

They didn't talk much about the eviction for the next couple of days, but for Raúl, it was the subtext of every conversation. "I guess I'll be homeless," he said one afternoon.

When push came to shove, a few days before eviction day, Ernesto relented. "Of course, I wanted my brother to come live with me," he told me. "Obviously." He'd just been kidding all along. He was sure Raúl had known that.

We stuffed Raúl's possessions into garbage bags and grocery totes. A cracked DVD, batteries, a razor, deodorant. Raúl scooped up a pile of thin, polished wooden sticks—a disassembled easel, he explained, for the paintings he would like to start doing. It had stood in his room ready at attention, empty. "You should have seen the paintings I used to do in El Salvador," he said. "I was really, really good."

We were taking his things to Ernesto's before school.

"Say goodbye to your house!" I said cheerily, trying to lighten the mood.

"I'm coming back later today to clean it," he replied in monotone, "before work."

The parking lot was filled with families corralling little children with lunch boxes into their cars and toward the bus. I reversed, getting out of everyone's way. We drove slowly by the ordinary yet spectacular sight of mothers taking their kids to school.

CHAPTER 15

By the summer of 2015, the twins were living on their own. Things settled into a rhythm. They had steady jobs, the weather was warm but not too hot, and they were excelling at summer school. The school days ended at two o'clock, instead of three-thirty. That extra hour and a half allowed them more time to relax with friends before heading to Montclair.

Raúl, in particular, was grateful for the routine. Those days of uncertainty between the eviction notice and Ernesto allowing him to move in had shaken him deeply. Sometimes he felt like the bad spirits that seemed to stalk him lay below the surface, dormant, but there inside him.

"I've got a bomb inside my head," he said. "I can feel it in there. It's like I can hear it clicking."

Their parents needed money worse than ever. The debt was nearly twenty thousand dollars now, and things had gotten bad in the fields. "There's a drought," his father explained. The summer of 2015 was a terribly dry one in El Salvador. In just June and July, more than one hundred million dollars in revenue from corn alone was lost, affecting about 211,000 acres, mostly from small-scale farming operations like the Flores family's.

They were almost through the spring's harvest, and Wilber Sr. worried about the rest of the year. "We're suffering, *mijo*," he said to Raúl. "We just haven't had any rain." Since living alone the twins had sent $200, $500, and $750 installments, but they still couldn't crack the goal of a thousand a month.

Every month Maricela walked to visit the moneylender and offer excuses. Sometimes Wilber Sr. went along with her. It was shameful, admitting again and again that they couldn't pay.

Raúl and Ernesto remembered the time after Wilber Jr. left, when the whole family had huddled together in the kitchen, stomachs rumbling, eight children listening to their mother and father spin lies about how they were all good, just fine, that Wilber shouldn't worry, no problem if he couldn't send money that month, may God bless him. That now his parents were openly telling Raúl and Ernesto about their woes meant it had to be bad—really bad. He and Ernesto scrounged together what they could and sent seventy-five dollars the next day. It wasn't much, but it was something. Their guilt ate away at them in pieces.

• • •

Meanwhile, turmoil raged in their home country.

On Monday, July 27, 2015, early morning commuters waited along the road for their rides throughout El Salvador. Cars and buses hurtled down streets. Over the weekend country-wide murmurings had begun: there was going to be a *paro,* halt—a forced bus strike. According to the Revolucionarios branch of the Barrio 18 gang, any bus driver who went to work on Monday would risk being shot and killed. The government had mobilized police and army officials to guard the buses that did run.

Many bus drivers stayed home. The news reports filtered in through the radio and television and streetside buzz: by day's end, five bus drivers and one transit worker were dead.

Thousands of commuters who'd made it to work that morning had no way to get home to their families.

The gangs had targeted the transit system for years, extorting money out of drivers and killing those who didn't pay. But this was the first country-wide action of this kind. They wanted the government to ease up on its anti-gang crackdown. The Barrio 18 splinter group was sending a message: *We own you. We can rip out the roots of commerce in an instant.*

It continued like this on Tuesday, Wednesday. Businesses closed since people couldn't go to work. And the people whose family economy relied on selling their goods by the bus stops—bags of fruit, bottles of water, tortillas, chips, packages of fried plantains—had no one to sell to. Some schools and universities suspended classes. The Salvadoran newspaper *El Diario de Hoy* reported that twelve million dollars in commerce was lost each day of the strike, from roadside *pupusa* vendors all the way up to the country's largest companies.

Tuesday evening: President Salvador Sánchez Cerén made a public address, promising more security forces to bolster the transportation workers and civil society against the gangs' threats. They wouldn't negotiate anymore, Sánchez Cerén insisted. "The criminals want to hold talks, but we can't talk with those who live by killing and extortion," he said.

Wednesday morning: President Sánchez Cerén left on a preplanned trip to get medical care in Cuba and wouldn't return for nearly two weeks. He did not change his plans.

Early that morning, traffic was particularly bad going into the city limits from the east. There had been an accident, it seemed. A bus hit a tree, perhaps, and rolled onto its side. The area was roped off by caution tape, blocking most of the inbound lanes. Later a news announcement stated that the bus accident was, in fact, a crime scene. A Barrio 18 gangster had boarded the bus at a popular stop and fired a round of bullets at the twenty-one-year-old driver, killing him on the spot.

Rumors trembled through the streets, everyone grasping for some kind of explanation. Were the rival gangs, in fact, working together on this strike? Was ARENA, the conservative party and rival to the president's FMLN, actually behind it? Could ARENA have been encouraging the army to boycott going to work, thus upending the government order?

In a cryptic moment of Tuesday's speech, the president asked ARENA to stop destabilizing the government. To what was he referring? Was he just trying to deflect criticism on his handling of the strike onto the opposition? Was the president in fact dying and in need of urgent medical care, hence his trip to Cuba during this crisis? None of these questions were confirmed fact, much of them baseless, but they were suspicions nonetheless.

Thursday, Friday, the same. By the following Wednesday, it seemed the stoppage had come to a close, but then again the news reports trickled in: another bus driver had been shot and killed. The country had lost well more than sixty million dollars in commerce. And the gangs? Everyone could see how powerful they were.

The twins were lucky to be away from the violence and corruption sweeping El Salvador that summer. But problems were also arising in the States. They didn't know much about the US government, but ever since the rich guy who wanted to be president started talking about building a wall and deporting immigrants home, the Spanish news stations, and the whole Latino community they knew—from their friends at school, to their coworkers, to the lady who cut their hair for cheap—were talking about Donald Trump.

"Do you know he said Mexicans were rapists and criminals?" Raúl said.

"Asshole," said Ernesto. In the evenings the restaurant kitchens were filled with chatter about this guy, his racism. The kitchen crews at both restaurants laughed about the things he'd said as they scrubbed the pans and stacked the dishes into the sinks—"We'll all go home, boys! Donald Trump's on his way!" But, both twins noted, real fear underlay the joking.

A lot of people on the news and at school said he wouldn't win the nomination, but most of their friends and coworkers weren't so sure.

"I think he'll win," Raúl said. "Definitely." People were racist, he knew, and lots of people in the United States— even in Oakland—disliked immigrants. They could feel it, sometimes, in the gazes of people in the pizza shop or the *taquería* by school; that look reserved for people thought of as outsiders and even as threats. What had immigrants ever done to them, besides build their houses, pick their food in the fields, serve it to them in restaurants, wash their plates, then do it all over again? Or besides sharing their cultural, culinary, and creative contributions with their communities. Let alone simply being fellow humans who deserved respect.

"He will be the president," Raúl insisted, and then, "we'll all have to watch out."

The twins had a three-week break between the end of summer classes and the start of the 2015 school year, which offered a gift of time: they could sleep in as late as they wanted and see friends in the mornings and afternoons. But soon enough it was back to long nights and too-early mornings. After a week in the twelfth grade, where they understood little and couldn't keep up with the work, they made a decision: they wanted to try eleventh grade over again.

"We want to focus this time," Ernesto told the school counselor.

A week later the twins received the good news, right on time given the political anxiety: their green cards, said Amy, had finally arrived.

"I'll believe it when I have it in my own hands," Raúl said.

Ernesto worked seven days a week while Raúl worked five, so it was Raúl who went into San Francisco to pick up the cards. He was giddy. What would they look like?

In her office, Amy handed the cards over with a smile. "You don't want to lose this," she said. "But you really should carry it around with you, just in case you're ever picked up for any reason." It was rare but wasn't unheard of, she explained, for the authorities to put someone in immigration detention, only to later figure out that that person had papers.

Now that they had their *papeles,* they could get passports, which meant they would legally be able to travel—and visit El Salvador. This was an option Wilber had never had.

On the one hand things back home were terrible and getting worse. In addition to the debt and the drought, homicides were higher than even before the 2012 truce. The MS-13 and Barrio 18 factions were at war as always, but now the government was ramping up its side of things. Following the bus strike, El Salvador's Supreme Court ruled that any gang member was to be, in the eyes of the law, considered a terrorist and thus subject to even harsher prison sentences. The street wars were out of control, with nearly thirty homicides a day in August—higher even than during the civil war.

On the other hand the twins missed their family.

But plane fare was expensive. It would only be a consideration for that magic, future time when their debt would be settled.

The twins argued over which place was better: the United States or El Salvador. Raúl insisted the United States was better, but Ernesto, the one who had lusted for life up north, now wasn't so sure.

"It's safe here," Raúl insisted, throwing his hands up. "I'll never go back there, not ever!"

"It's dangerous here, too!" Ernesto reminded him. Oakland had plenty of violence of its own; they had both been jumped, after all.

Yes, there was violence in Oakland, allowed Raúl, but nothing like in El Salvador.

"Things are fine," Esperanza told her boys when they next called, back to whitewashing the narrative. "Things are fine. We pray for you, my angels."

Being in the United States spared the twins the pressure of joining a gang in their home country. It also spared them the danger of being *suspected* of being a gang member there. A Salvadoran law called *agrupación ilícita,* or illicit congregation, allows law enforcement to arrest anyone who looks suspicious, which often means youth dressed stylishly and hanging out together in public spaces. They are assumed to be guilty of being in a gang, without proof or a trial.

These efforts are part of an Iron Fist campaign, a reaction, in part, to the failed truce of 2012, which began to unravel in 2014. Police patrols are on the rise, and several illegal killings of suspected gang members—extrajudicial massacres that smack of the death squad atrocities of the civil war years—have been exposed by local press, who risk payback from both the corrupt police *and* the gangs. A Salvadoran young person risks becoming a target on both sides of the law.

In recent years Salvadoran individuals and businesses, from market vendors to *pupusa* shops to hotels, have paid an estimated $756 million in *renta*. The increments are often small—twenty, fifty, two hundred dollars every two weeks—and paid for protection from the very people who collect it. And still most gangsters remain small-time, barely eking out a living.

The violence has increased over the years, and the sheer number of gang members seems to be growing, too, though it's complicated to count. In 2013, a thorough but unscientific study by the Salvadoran government estimated that there were 470,000 Salvadorans—more than 7 percent of the population—with direct ties to gangs.

El Salvador has nowhere to put all the suspected criminals. In 2015, prisons reached 310 percent of intended capacity; holding cells that were meant for temporary confinement are crammed with young men, and sometimes women, who can spend months and even years awaiting trial.

For the Flores twins the first practical order of business, after getting their green cards, was to apply for Social Security cards. Getting those would mean the Floreses could start working for full minimum wage.

Paperwork in hand—birth certificates, completed applications, and green cards—they went to an office building in downtown Oakland, where the doorman directed them to the third floor. They sat down to wait among the rows of gray metal seats.

An hour later, when their number was finally called, they handed their materials to the officer behind the counter.

"Twins, huh?" the woman said, looking them over. Same faces, both dressed in their common uniform of black shirts, jeans, and red-and-black Nikes. She scanned their paperwork.

"Okay, whose is this?" she asked, waving Ernesto's birth certificate.

"Mine," he said.

"This one I can do, but yours," she said, pointing to Raúl, "I need an original." She shook his birth certificate. Ernesto had a tattered color copy with a new stamp, so it looked original, whereas Raúl's was a black-and-white facsimile, the duplication slightly askew.

"Come back when you have it," she said matter-of-factly, and thrust the copy back, moving on with Ernesto's application. Raúl nodded and stepped away from the counter, not daring to argue.

When Ernesto's Social Security card arrived at school six days later, he laughed as he tore open the envelope. When he saw the small card attached by perforation, "That's it?" he said. This thing everyone wanted, that people bought and traded on the black market, that ensured fair wages and employability, looked like something he could have made in computer class. He'd take it that night to his boss and get on the official payroll.

Raúl left the room.

Ernesto was doing well at work. He did less dishwashing and more busing now, working invisibly around the customers. He even answered the phone every now and then, something he secretly loved to do. "Hello, how can I help you?" he'd say in English that, though his vocabulary remained limited, was less and less accented each day. His boss complimented him on his work ethic and made sure he was tipped out at the end of each night. Wilber Sr. had taught his children to work hard. It wasn't easy, said Ernesto, to find such hard workers as he and his brother.

The customers liked him, too. A few regulars would slip his tips into the pocket of his apron.

"I get a lot of attention from women customers," Ernesto explained to me. "I think it's because I wear a shirt with short sleeves, and I carry a lot of things, which flexes my muscles so it makes me look like I'm really strong."

He felt welcome, needed, and capable at the sushi

restaurant. In most other Montclair establishments, he felt out of place. They were *gabacho* restaurants, restaurants for white people, for Americans—not for people like him and his brother. "I'm embarrassed," he said, just walking into a *gabacho* place. "I don't feel comfortable in places like that." In many ways he had painfully digested and internalized the racism against Latinos that surrounded them.

Raúl felt it too. Not that they were born different, but they grew up different and therefore were different—it was a cultural thing. "Places like that," from the twins' point of view, were where people like them worked, not where they were patrons. Their comfort in the affluent parts of Oakland wasn't an issue of either language or legality. Living on the margins of a gentrifying city only underlined to Ernesto what the twins had been told and had fought their whole lives: that they were less than, and that they didn't, and shouldn't expect to, belong.

One night at the restaurant Ernesto took a photo with Jerry Brown, the governor of California, who was dining there. He thanked Brown in English and turned toward the kitchen, right then posting the photo to Instagram and Snapchat, overlaid with the caption "With the governor," followed by a blushing emoji.

On a busy night a few weeks later, Ernesto was busing the table of a couple in their twenties, perspiring in his smeared black apron. The table was a mess of splattered soy sauce and sushi remnants, and Ernesto did his best to be inconspicuous as he cleared the plates. The guy had ordered several large beers already. He gesticulated just as Ernesto went to take one of his empty bottles, inadvertently swatting it out of Ernesto's hands and into his own lap.

"Fucking Latino!" he shouted.

Ernesto narrowed his eyes and said back, "Fuck you!"

The guy moved as if to hit Ernesto, who didn't flinch, but then his girlfriend calmed him down. Ernesto turned around and walked toward the kitchen. He punched a wall in the back of the restaurant and dented it slightly, ripping the skin off his knuckles. His boss didn't reprimand him but simply said, "Stay in the back until he's gone."

CHAPTER 16

Ernesto dreamed of going home.

He knew he couldn't go to La Colonia—too dangerous—but he could at least get to the capital and meet his mother there, maybe his father and some of his siblings, too. *Someday,* he thought.

Raúl, for his part, still had no interest in going back. He had been dwelling in the past again; if he allowed himself to think too much, his whole body began to shake. That place had kicked him out on his ass, far away from his family, his loved ones, his place, his future.

Raúl felt this anger, but also, he could admit sometimes, a fear. "I'm scared," he said, to go back. People he'd trusted had let him down spectacularly.

He finally received his Social Security card, but as the fall dragged on, his anxiety mounted. He had a hard time sleeping, and even when he was awake, thoughts rose to the surface that for more than a year had been pretty well tamped down. He'd be sitting on a bus or in class, and it would suddenly go black all around him, as if he were there on the cold roadside in Guatemala, head throbbing and listening to the *coyota* scream. Now that he was truly "safe" in the United States, all the old worries and soiled memories came flooding back in.

Meanwhile, Ernesto fell in love. It was a good distraction from both homesickness and bad memories. His new girlfriend was a ninth grader; too young for him, Ernesto knew. Sofía was her name. Ernesto loved her eyes; sultry but also kind and soft. Though she was only fourteen, she had a lot of responsibilities at home, where she had to cook and clean and take care of little kids. She understood him, he felt.

Best of all she was from El Salvador.

Raúl was jealous. He also wasn't sure about Sofía. She'd chat with other boys, sometimes not even acknowledge the twins as they passed. And then she'd go accusing Ernesto of flirting with other girls on Facebook and complaining about how he spent too much time working.

Sofía buddied up to Raúl at first, calling him her *cuñado,* her in-law. Sofía didn't seem to have a hard time telling them apart, even from the beginning. Raúl liked that about her. But Sofía monopolized his brother's attention. During lunch, Ernesto and Sofía would snuggle on the couch in the back of the library while Raúl sat alone with his earbuds and phone.

Raúl could feel the bomb in his head making him jittery and withdrawn, but his brother didn't seem to notice. He had been there for Ernesto the year before when he was unraveling—all those nightmares and breakdowns. Now his twin was off with this fourteen-year-old, and he'd become invisible.

Maricela continued to hound her brothers. "How much can you send this month? We're worried they're going to take away the land for real this time." She asked them about school—how much longer until they graduated? Could they take a break?

"We only go to school a couple of hours a day," Raúl told her, which was a lie. "We're doing everything we can."

Cesar remained a steadfast father and boyfriend, sending seventy dollars each month, visiting La Colonia as often as he could, meeting Maricela outside the factory on his lunch break. She'd ride more than an hour each way to see him for this fleeting break, but it was worth it.

Cesar complained all the time about how bad his job was. He worked hard at that factory, tiring his body and wasting his mind, all for practically no money. After a few months the owners cut everyone's hours, and thus their wages, so he only made $350. He was starting to think that the way out was the United States. Once he figured out how to get papers, he said, he'd get them for Maricela and the kids, too.

Complicating matters, both Wilber Sr. and Esperanza had recently contracted chikungunya, a mosquito-borne virus not unlike dengue fever that wipes people out for weeks with a fever, sore muscles, and aching joints. They were barely able to get out of bed to use the bathroom. Though rarely fatal, the greatest risk of chikungunya is to infants and the elderly—like Wilber Sr., only in his sixties, but weakened, it seemed, by his fears around losing the land. Maricela sponged her parents' brows and spoonfed them soup and *atole,* a corn porridge, as she thought over Cesar's plan. Her father had grown alarmingly frail. At times, staring at him on the bed like that, sweating, stiff, his chest hardly rising and falling, she worried he might die. And what would happen to their family then?

Maricela finally gave Cesar her blessing to go; she was convinced because he was convinced. She also started to think about going north herself—for real this time.

Over time, Cesar set the plan to go north aside.

Still, Maricela thought about going.

"Don't come," Ernesto messaged her on Facebook. "Seriously. Don't do it." She scrolled through their photos again. If she were in their place, everything would be different—not just for her, but for the whole family. It should have been she who'd gone.

"We'll see," she replied.

Going all that way by herself without a *coyote* would be too risky. Many women, she knew, were raped, kidnapped, and even killed. She'd have to go with a *coyote,* which cost about eight thousand dollars these days. Could her family take out another loan, this time in her own name?

. . .

In 2012, El Salvador had the highest rate of femicide—the gender-motivated killing of women—in the world. High femicide rates persist, and reports of rape and domestic violence are also on the rise. The vast majority of victims are poor young women living in rural areas or urban slums.

Is it so surprising that more and more girls are joining the gangs, wresting a tiny hunk of power from the male-dominated world—of gangs, of police, of the trials and tribulations of their own families—around them? Is it so surprising that more and more girls are going north, fleeing the dangers—sometimes with children in tow?

Gang members reserve the right to claim any girl in the neighborhood as a girlfriend, threatening her or her family with physical harm if she refuses to comply. Gang members' mothers, sisters, aunts, grandmothers, and spouses—who wash their clothes, cook their food, keep houses—are linked to the gangs sometimes without meaning or asking to be.

"Women often take the same risks for crimes as the men do," explains Silvia Juárez, of the Organization of Salvadoran Women for Peace (ORMUSA), "but they don't receive the same revenue or benefit of the crime."

The fact is that young women in El Salvador don't have a lot of options. According to a 2015 study by the United Nations Population Fund (UNFPA), around a third of all pregnancies in El Salvador were girls or young women between the ages of ten and nineteen. Twenty-five percent of girls are married before they are eighteen, and abortion is illegal; women in El Salvador have been jailed for even having a miscarriage. Salvadoran girls attend school at approximately the same rates as boys, yet schooling is subpar for all. More than three hundred thousand youth in El Salvador are currently out of school and without a job.

A paralegal working with unaccompanied minors in the Rio Grande Valley of Texas explains that girls know what they're risking on the trip north. "They take the pill or get a birth control shot so that, if they are raped, they won't get pregnant." A 2010 Amnesty International report cited research that six out of ten migrant women and girls were sexually assaulted en route to the United States—other estimates are even higher.

In October, Raúl decided that he wouldn't go to school anymore. A few of their friends, like Ibrahim and Diego, had graduated. Others, like Douglas and Alfredo, had dropped out or switched schools. They hadn't really kept in touch. Being around people, friends new and old, now made Raúl anxious, and besides, he wanted to be with his own girlfriend. He'd met Marleny on Kik. She was a senior at a high school downtown, and though she was born in the United States, she was Mexican American and had grown up speaking Spanish. Like him, she was tired of school, and like him, she was lonely.

The Monday after they started going out, Raúl and Marleny ditched together. They met up in downtown Oakland and walked the streets, relishing the freedom of having nowhere to be and being in love. They sat on the benches in Jefferson Square Park, halfway between the city center and the highway, and hopped another bus to the lake, where they walked its perimeter, holding hands. They made out before they hopped on the bus and ate tacos on International Boulevard. When he left for work in Montclair, he promised to see her the next day.

Around the time he met Marleny, he began cutting himself. He'd heard of kids at school doing this, how sometimes people felt better with a little bit of pain. He tried it once, and the feeling of the blood seeping from his skin was like a release.

As Ernesto was sleeping one night, Raúl took out a small knife, hunched over by the light of a lamp on his bed, and sliced.

Ernesto woke up. "What are you doing?" he hissed.

"Leave me alone. It makes me feel better." But he was glad Ernesto was awake as he cut more slashes into his arm, digging just deep enough to let out a satisfying bit of blood, just enough to start beading on the skin. The accumulation would linger a moment and then burst its own dam, dripping down his arm in a stream just red and thick enough to be impressive.

For a week he passed the time like this: leaving with Ernesto in the morning with the promise of going back to school, getting on the bus, then jumping off downtown to meet Marleny before Ernesto could stop him. Raúl didn't care that he was lying to Ernesto every time he promised to go to school.

But after that first week, Marleny insisted she needed to go back to class—it was her senior year, and she loved him, but she had to be in school. For her *future*. So after their morning meet-up, he began dropping her off in front of her school, then chose a bus to hop on. One took him to Alameda, where he stared out the window as the bus crossed the Oakland estuary and meandered through the quiet, tree-lined streets full of big houses. Another took him to the base of the Oakland hills, where he looked up at the hillsides balding from thirst—the same drought, he knew, that was afflicting his family back in El Salvador. For another week he rode AC Transit to new places, not answering his brothers' phone calls, not answering anyone's calls; just staring out the window, feeling his arm throb, listening to the tick-tock in his head.

Marleny was the only one he wanted to talk to, but after not too long, their relationship turned tense. He resented her for not skipping with him and accused her of having another boyfriend in school; she accused him of flirting with other girls. Twice that third week they broke up and got back together again.

Raúl spent nearly two weeks under the radar, avoiding school and his twin. He added more piercings to his face like more and more of his friends had at school, loving the way the needle felt when it pushed through his skin. He changed the barbell of the eyebrow piercing on his right side to a peg with black shiny barbs on each end, then added a twin piercing on the left side, which gave the impression of horns. Ernesto already had an eyebrow piercing, but now Raúl had two. Ernesto had pierced his upper cheek, but Raúl bested him again, piercing a pinch of flesh on his temple, opting for barbed ends on that one too. The last and most expensive piercing was a little circle that clipped into his cheek like a small, sparkling shield. Ernesto didn't have anything like that.

On the bus after each piercing, Raúl would polish the screen of his phone and hold it up as a mirror, admiring the work. He felt proud of the way he was designing himself. It was a free country here. No one would bother him for these piercings or assume he was a gang member, as they might back home—just as they might for his Nikes, his clothes.

He never once missed work. He'd end each sojourn at the Italian restaurant, always showing up just before his five o'clock shift so he could change into his work clothes—a T-shirt stained and stretched at the neckline, dishwater-soiled pants—pull on his thick white apron, and get to work on the dishes.

The older guys at the restaurant called him Pepito and poked fun at him for being the youngest, but he didn't care. He knew he was the best worker, and for those six hours every night, he took refuge in efficiency—every moment meant more of a dollar he could take home, every dish a concrete task. It was when he was walking, or lying in bed, or looking out the window on the bus, that the bomb came back into his head. Maricela had called a few nights earlier to report that Esperanza and Wilber Sr. had come down with chikungunya; he hated that he wasn't there to help them. He was stuck here in Oakland where he didn't really want to be, but he would never go back, either.

. . .

"What the fuck?" Ernesto said in English when he saw Raúl's new piercings.

"I can do whatever I want. It's my face," said Raúl.

"You're always following what I'm doing," Ernesto replied.

"Fuck you. I make my own choices." They didn't talk the rest of that night.

They were careful not to post too many close-ups on Facebook so their siblings wouldn't see their piercings and tattle to their parents. Wilber Sr. and Esperanza would think it was devil work, if not proof that they'd become gangsters up north.

That weekend Ernesto got a new barb on his eyebrow, then a half ring on his lip. Sofía thought they were cool, but after the lip ring, she thought things had gone far enough. "No more," she said.

After a month of going out together, Ernesto decided it was time to ask Sofía's parents for permission to date her. This was a common custom: a young man courting a girl must ask her parents for approval.

He hadn't approached Sofía's mother yet because Sofía wasn't allowed to date anyone until her fifteenth birthday, which was coming up. Ernesto was planning to ask soon afterward, but he was nervous. He rehearsed in his head: he'd take out all his piercings, visit her home, and look her parents in the eye with stiff formality: "I am your daughter's boyfriend, and I want to ask your permission to keep seeing her. I love her very much, and it's not right for us to go on without your permission." What worried him was the questions they might ask—about his age, his family, where he lived, whom he lived with, his grades in school. He knew he couldn't give reassuring answers to these.

She wanted him to be at her *quinceañera,* her fifteenth birthday celebration, but it was a Saturday on Halloween weekend, and getting off work would be hard. She flip-flopped between understanding and being annoyed that her boyfriend couldn't come to her party, her big day. He'd do his best, he told her.

He focused on her real birthday, two weeks before the party. That day he carried a bouquet of "Happy Birthday" balloons to school, along with a necklace and matching earrings that he'd carefully picked out from Forever 21. He felt sure she'd like the attention of getting jewelry and a bunch of balloons from her boyfriend in public. But he was more than an hour late to school, and before he could find her, she sent an angry string of texts: "You're not a responsible person." "It's my birthday and you don't even come on time to see me." "You don't take school seriously."

They spent the day in a fight. He shoved the balloons toward her and walked off. She snatched their ribbons before they floated away.

"Maybe we'll break up," he told Raúl later, shrugging. He didn't want that. But he was too tired to fight. After hours of back-and-forth texting that night, they made up. "Thank you for my balloons," she said. The next day he gave her the jewelry. When she untied the bow and lifted the top of the box, she squealed and hugged him. He gently hung the necklace around her, fastening it from behind, and she clipped on the earrings eagerly. They were good again.

• • •

Raúl and Marleny broke up for good. Ernesto worried about what Raúl did all day, and also about his parents laid up back home, shaking with fever. They'd been sick now for more than two weeks with chikungunya. "You don't understand," he told me when I tried to reassure him. "They're old, and frail. This could kill them."

Raúl started posting photographs of his cut-up arms online. "What is he doing to himself?" Ernesto said. "If my mother knew, she'd just— I don't know what, she'd die."

One morning when Ernesto couldn't take it anymore, he left school to go look for Raúl downtown. Ernesto dialed his twin's number on repeat, in hopes of driving him crazy enough to answer. He pictured his brother watching the phone ring and ring and ring, flashing his name. Raúl had never ignored him like this.

He'd heard the stories before, in El Salvador and here, the stuff of bad movies and bad dreams: "All of a sudden you get a phone call, and your brother is dead." Suicide, he meant.

Ernesto took to camping out in my office, overwhelmed, looking for help tracking down Raúl. One day a group of Yemeni mothers, clad in long, shiny black abayas that covered their frames from wrist to neck to ankle, and colorful scarves pinned tightly against their faces, visited the office regarding the parent English class we offered. They noticed Ernesto seated in the corner and murmured to one another in Arabic. They wanted to know what had happened to this sad boy.

189

"What's wrong?" one of them asked him. "Are you okay?"

Where to start? He shook his head, then replied, "My mom is sick."

"Your mama is sick? Oh, is she in the hospital?" the woman asked.

"No, she's in El Salvador."

"You're here in this country all by yourself without your mama?"

"Where's your dad?"

"He's in El Salvador too."

"*Habibi,* sorry, you poor baby," the woman said, looking at Ernesto with tenderness. Then all four of the women teared up, seemingly surprised at their own sudden outpouring of emotion, missing their own families at home, perhaps, and dabbing their eyes with tissues and the ends of their head scarves and whispering to one another.

Ernesto tensed his jaw and swiveled his chair toward the corner. Seeing them there, these four women with their kind faces, made Ernesto miss Esperanza even more, and he began to cry. He hadn't cried in a long time; even when he had been unraveling last spring, when he'd gotten the racing heart and trouble breathing, he'd never cried—not while sober, anyway. The horrible traumas that had happened to him had once ruled him; now life was relatively good for him, but had become terrible for everyone else he loved. The tears came fast and hard. He twisted his face to stop them, but it was no use—they just kept coming, and the more they came, the more he felt like a boy and remembered crying in his mother's arms, the way he could let his whole body fall into hers.

The truth was, he needed Raúl as much as Raúl needed him. But how could he help him? He wanted to be angry, but he could feel only love and worry for the person he was closest to in the world. He hunched toward the wall and let it go, filling the room with the echoes of his grief.

The women wiped their faces and stood up to go. "We'll pray for you," said the one who spoke English. "*Habibi*, we'll pray for you."

"Thank you," he managed. She'd spoken in English, and he'd understood what she'd said.

Raúl had missed nine days in a row of school.

"Do you know what happened today?" Ernesto said to him after work that night. "I was in Ms. Lauren's office, and a bunch of Arab ladies came in and asked about Mom. And I cried. I fucking cried—because of you."

Raúl was surprised. He knew his brother was concerned, but not this much.

"I'm scared you're going to end up dead," Ernesto said. "I don't want to be crying in a room full of ladies because I don't know where you are, or what's going on, and you're not even picking up your phone."

"I know," Raúl said. "I'm sorry."

"If you don't quit that," Ernesto said, pointing to Raúl's scabby forearms, "I'm going to kick your ass." He told his brother, "I love you," after a pause.

The next day Raúl came back to school.

CHAPTER 17

It was an accident, of course. A broken condom. Sofía and Ernesto had had sex only a few times. They planned to buy the morning-after pill, which they'd learned about in school, but they hadn't made it to the drugstore—they didn't have enough money on hand, and she had no time to slip out of the house unnoticed—until two days later. She took the pill, and they figured it would still work.

During the December holiday break, the twins slept in, relishing the time off. Some mornings Sofía and Ernesto met up in Fruitvale and got food, Ernesto always footing the bill, and walked around the neighborhood holding hands. She was the first girlfriend with whom he'd had an ongoing intimate relationship, and though he knew their age difference made sex against the law, he didn't turn down the opportunity. He loved her.

Ernesto and Raúl had taken on more hours at work, and

they made a new plan to deal with the debt: every two-week pay period they would each lay away $250 and wouldn't touch it, so that by the end of the month, they would have saved a thousand dollars to send home. Even better was the news that Oakland's minimum wage was going up again: when the clock struck midnight on December 31, they'd be making $12.55 an hour, a thirty-cent increase. That could add up.

"For real?" Maricela wrote when they told her that a large sum was coming their way. Right before the new year, they sent $1,100 back to El Salvador. If they stuck with the plan—difficult but not impossible—they could unburden the family of the whole debt within a couple of years.

In mid-January they had five hundred dollars laid away from their January 1 paychecks. School was back in session.

But Sofía wasn't feeling that well. "I think I'm pregnant," she told Ernesto.

She seemed serious. He bought her a test. The pill hadn't worked; Sofía was pregnant.

They didn't talk about their options—they didn't see any other choice but her keeping the baby. "I would never give my baby away to anyone else," Sofía said. And neither of them thought to consider getting an abortion—it was illegal in El Salvador, and so something they just wouldn't think to do. They'd be keeping it.

"Sofía's pregnant," he told Raúl a few days after finding out, with a tremor in his voice.

Raúl didn't respond at first. "You're an idiot."

Ernesto nodded. He was so overwhelmed, he could do nothing else.

"What were you thinking?" Raúl laid into Ernesto just as Ernesto had laid into Maricela. Didn't Ernesto know how much harder he had just made everything?

Meanwhile, back home, Maricela began to develop some suspicions about Cesar. What she considered her female intuition wouldn't let it go. Something was up.

Finally he told her. "I'm staying with someone else," he said. A woman.

Cesar had been back in touch with an old girlfriend from long ago. She lived on her own, and he stayed over there more often until he decided, lovesick and wanting to get out of his parents' house, to move in with her. That was that. One day he was a devoted father and loving husband-to-be to Maricela, and the next he was cheating with this woman from his past.

Things were meant to be different this time around, and yet here she was again. The news of his affair knocked the wind out of her, and stuck in La Colonia, she had no way to intervene or to stop them.

Things happen. People fall in love with other people. A man could vanish from his commitments in a heartbeat, take on a new life. For men the world was always open. Not so, thought Maricela, for women. Who would love her now? She walked around the dark house in La Colonia slumped with heartbreak, checking her phone constantly in hopes that it might offer a reversal of fate.

The phone didn't ring. He'd blocked her online. He

didn't respond to her calls, her pleading text messages. It was over.

After a few nights of fitful sleep, she came to the conclusion that this girl must be working witchcraft on Cesar. *Brujería*. How else could a man change like that, on a dime?

Cesar's mom was on Maricela's side. "Come down here, and we'll talk about it," she said. They'd find a way to get Cesar back in his right mind. Maricela felt reassured as she listened, but as soon as she hung up the phone, the doubt settled in like old dust.

Ernesto hadn't even asked Sofía's mom and stepdad for permission to date her, and now they had to tell them about the pregnancy.

Sofía didn't want to do it alone. "You're the dad, and you need to be there when I tell them," she said.

Ernesto knew she was right. He hadn't told anyone about the baby besides Raúl.

"We have to do it tomorrow," Sofía texted.

Ernesto agreed. "Will you come with me?" he asked Raúl. Raúl looked at him like he was crazy.

"Please?" Ernesto said, his tone uncharacteristically pleading.

"Okay," Raúl agreed with a shrug.

Ever since that night Ernesto had laid into him, he had stopped cutting his arms and ditching school, though his fog of depression hadn't lifted. But now that Ernesto had his own personal emergency, Raúl rose to the occasion.

The only time Ernesto had come face-to-face with Sofía's mother before was at the *quinceañera*, which Ernesto had made it to, after all. Sofía had been dressed like a cake-top princess, and Ernesto showed up in a flaming red shirt and red Nikes, and piercings all over his face. *Puro marero,* Sofía's mom had told her after the party. Total gangster.

"He's not!" Sofía had said. "He's a really good person, really responsible."

The twins took the bus together and followed Sofía through the door. She motioned for them to sit on the couch across from her mother, Katerine, who had been waiting for them.

"Mom," she said, "this is my boyfriend." Ernesto forced himself to look up at Sofía's mother. "And his brother." She gestured at Raúl.

"Hello," Ernesto said.

Katerine, sensing something was coming, didn't respond.

"I'm pregnant."

Katerine heaved a groan and dropped her head into her lap.

Sofía began to cry. "I'm sorry," she said, "I'm sorry."

Ernesto couldn't bring himself to say anything, not a word.

Katerine also began to cry, shaking her head. "You did this," she said, pointing a shaking finger at Ernesto. "This is your problem now," she spat at him. She pointed at Sofía's belly. "You are responsible for her and for your baby."

Ernesto nodded miserably as Katerine shouted. She had given birth to Sofía at fifteen and had always wanted a different life for her. Sofía's father had abandoned them, and she'd managed to get them to the United States. And now, in spite of all her efforts, the cycle was repeating.

"I know," he said in a near-whisper. Raúl just sat there, quiet.

Soon Ernesto and Raúl picked themselves up off the couch. Ernesto murmured words of apology and followed Raúl out the door.

He texted with Sofía during the whole bus ride to work. Her mom was still referring to Ernesto as a gangster, citing his piercings, his clothes. She had called him *maleducado*, Sofía said. Badly brought up.

This infuriated Raúl. That lady didn't know the Flores family; she couldn't talk that way about his twin. But Ernesto took the hit. He straightened in his seat. It was time to grow up, to get down to business, to accept responsibility for what had happened, and to face their uncertain future.

At school Sofía told Ernesto that her mom was fuming, alternating between shouting at her and ignoring her entirely, addressing her only about logistics like watching her little brother or attending a prenatal appointment.

"She told me she wasn't going to support the baby. That I'd have to get a job, and you'd have to pay for everything."

"I will," Ernesto said. "I will, I promise. I'll take care of everything." He feared her mother would kick her out any minute; but the minuscule room he shared with his twin brother was no place for a girl like Sofía, let alone a baby. He'd need to find a new place. But who would rent to two kids about to have a baby?

Sofía concocted a fantasy in which she and her older,

employed boyfriend could live together, support a new-born, and create a family without hardship. Ernesto knew it wasn't so easy. The average price at the time for a studio in Oakland was more than twelve hundred dollars a month, about the entirety of Ernesto's salary. And plus, if they got a studio, where would Raúl go?

"I have to be responsible," Ernesto repeated like a mantra.

Raúl watched his brother mull over the mess of possibilities and obstacles. His brother had been so stupid—so, so stupid—to add another responsibility, another set of circumstances in which he owed something to someone else. And Sofía was so young. But his fury subsided into concern as he saw how the stress of it all weighed on his twin.

"I'll help you find a place," Raúl told him. "Whatever you do is fine with me."

The twins sent only four hundred dollars home in January. In February they sent nothing. They couldn't tell their parents about the baby—not yet.

Wilber Sr. had made it through chikungunya, but he was still achy and had low energy, and the instability of the land weakened him further. The creditors had told the Flores family that they'd put one of the parcels of land up for sale unless they brought in some cash.

The whole family worried that any minute, Wilber Sr. would die from the very idea of losing their land. The debt was likely to eat the Flores family alive.

. . .

Maricela hadn't received child support from Cesar in two months—he'd abandoned not only her but their daughter too. She went to file a report so that he would be ordered to resume payments. As a matter of procedure, she had to go to his workplace to get paperwork signed by his employers. She had the jitters as she rode the bus there, terrified at the thought of running into him, masochistically hopeful that she would. She knew the odds were practically none that she'd see him. And yet there, as she walked in the gate, was Cesar.

They both stopped.

She wasn't going to be the first one to talk.

"Aren't you going to hug me?" he asked.

"Why would I do that?"

"I'm sorry," he said.

She said nothing.

"Forgive me?" he pleaded. "I don't know what I was thinking. Forgive me. I love you. Take me back."

The other woman was now long gone. He regretted everything, he insisted. He'd only really left because he was confused and needed to get out of his parents' house. Maricela was the only woman in the world for him.

"I have to think about it," she said. "How can I ever trust you again?"

If she took him back—and though it was hard to admit, she wanted to—she knew it would never be the same.

"I know," he said. "I'm sorry. I'm so sorry."

She was proud of how stoic she stayed as he told her all the things she'd wanted to hear. She repeated that she'd think it over.

After a few days she agreed.

They went to San Salvador together to buy a promise ring—not an engagement ring, but a preengagement ring, a symbol of commitment. They walked out of the store happy. She couldn't stop stealing glances at her hand: the hand of a loved woman, of an almost-wife.

They kissed there in the street.

In Oakland, Sofía and Ernesto went to visit a school for teen moms, where Sofía might transfer. The school, run by the Alameda County Office of Education, partnered with Head Start to offer free childcare so that young mothers could earn their high school credits more quickly while also learning parenting skills. The campus was on the basement level of a commercial building, but in spite of its almost hidden location, it had computers and teachers and kind staff. There was a day care center where the babies and toddlers spent their days while their mothers studied. The staff, Ernesto noted, seemed to really love the little ones, and each kid was cared for. A few of the childcare workers spoke Spanish. Ernesto spotted a boy and a girl dressed the same and holding hands.

"Twins!" one of the ladies told him, laughing. A good enough sign for Ernesto.

"I like it here," Sofía said. She'd start in the summer session.

On TV at work, and in videos online, they saw seas of white people chanting "Build the wall," over and over again. Wasn't a big wall, they thought, already built? People held up signs: NO AMNESTY FOR ILLEGALS. NO LEGAL = NO JOBS. THE SILENT MAJORITY IS WITH TRUMP. THANK YOU, LORD JESUS, FOR PRESIDENT TRUMP. I'M READY TO WORK ON THE WALL. CLOSE BORDERS NOW. DEPORT ILLEGAL ALIENS. He saw a video from the year before about a homeless Latino man in Boston who was beaten up and pissed on by two brothers. "Trump was right," the alleged perpetrator said. "All these illegals need to be deported."

Wilber had come to the United States when George Bush was president and watched as Obama—the guy who'd campaigned on hope—ramped up his deportations. And now Trump. Wilber told his brothers he wasn't all that surprised that a guy like this was making headlines. To him, Trump represented the dark but very real side of the United States, filled with subtleties of racism and classism and xenophobia that often only immigrants could see. It wasn't so much him but his rallies: those seas of people chanting to build the wall, cheering when he said he would deport millions. Wilber knew he might very well be included in those millions.

At least, Ernesto considered, his baby would be born here. His adopted, not-quite-yet home was a better place to start from scratch than El Salvador. His baby would be a citizen, would speak English, would even vote. He'd vote, too, one day, if he ever became a citizen—if he got that chance.

Ernesto skipped classes on Friday to pick up an extra shift at work. He didn't get to see Sofía that day. That weekend

Sofía avoided his calls and sent only curt texts. What was going on?

He got a message from a friend of a friend. Sofía had been making out with a kid named Mario, a tenth grader from El Salvador, right in the middle of the courtyard on Friday. Everyone, the snitch assured Ernesto, had seen.

With his child inside her growing belly, she'd cheated on him.

Fuming, he texted her: "You're a cheat, you're a liar."

They texted furiously until he decided to turn his phone off. He'd never, ever forgive her. He'd never take her back.

The next day she confronted him and begged for his forgiveness. "I'm sorry!" she said. "I don't know what I was thinking! I'm just overwhelmed. I'm so sorry. I made a mistake. You have to forgive me."

Holding back tears, he shook his head. "I'm going to talk to your mom and let her know that I'll support the baby," he said with a quivering voice. "But I won't support you."

He couldn't look at her. He stormed past her and sat on the curb outside school and put his head between his knees. He wailed like a little boy.

He reported to work that night and then went home, phone turned off. He avoided her at school the next day and the next.

"I didn't mean it!" she said, cornering him one day in the office. "I'm so sorry!"

He'd calmed down somewhat. "I'll talk to you," he said. "It's the right thing for the baby."

By that afternoon they were nuzzling each other in the courtyard, holding hands.

From then on Ernesto and Sofía were on-again, off-again. One day Ernesto would post:

Today King Ernest & Queen Sofía LOVE FOR EVER EVER.

Soon afterward he'd post:

Fuck Relationships, I'm Single.

It was hard for any of their friends to keep track. It was hard for them to keep track, too.

But Sofía and his baby needed him, he knew, and this outweighed their day-to-day drama. If it was hard for him, he could muster the maturity to see that it was a thousand times worse for her: fifteen years old, carrying a baby. He would never walk away from his child, but he would always have the option to do so. She never would.

CHAPTER 18

Ernesto decided he wasn't going to go back to school in the fall. Outwardly he was confident about his choice. He and Raúl had failed several classes because, between the late nights working and the ups and downs of depression, it had been hard to make it to school. Things would only get more complicated once the baby came. What was the point of being in school if he wasn't getting any closer to graduation? But his decision was a loss. By giving up his boyhood dream of a US education, he was both accepting the reality of his circumstances and falling on his sword.

The school counselor helped him enroll in the publicly funded adult school in nearby Alameda. There, he could take classes part-time to earn credits toward his high school diploma. He'd have more time to work, and he'd be able to pick up another job.

"We need to send money home," said Raúl.

"I have to focus on my family," he said. Sofía, he meant, and the baby.

"What about *our* family?"

"We just didn't know how hard it was going to be. We thought it was easier to make money." He was almost casual, Raúl felt, about abandoning his plans, his promises.

Raúl didn't have that kind of luxury. Now with Ernesto, like Wilber, focusing on his own small world, he'd have to assume the burden of the debt. Of saving the family.

At Sofía's baby shower, Raúl sat in the corner, silent. How much had this cost, he wondered. These games, these decorations, these gifts, all this food? How much had Ernesto contributed? Ernesto was aware that all the guests were Sofía's people, that he didn't know anyone except Raúl. And Raúl wondered if anyone would notice if he disappeared.

With Ernesto spending so much time with Sofía, Raúl reached out to Wilber. They hadn't spent much time with Wilber, and when they did hang out, he made clear that they'd have to pay for their own food or chip in for gas—even though he always paid for Gabby or friends of his who tagged along. The twins didn't mind paying, but it seemed like Wilber was trying to make a point, which made everything feel strained. Raúl called, anyway.

"Want to come running?" Wilber asked.

Wilber now ran every day. It calmed him, he said. Raúl had a hard time keeping up, but he admired his brother's discipline. He, too, had been working out: one hundred push-ups and one hundred sit-ups each night. Running through the hills like that was relaxing, Wilber felt. His anxiety had built of late: he was working a lot, growing tired of the commute, fighting with Gabby. He worried about what he was hearing on the news.

Ernesto hadn't told Wilber about the baby, and Raúl kept the secret.

When it came time for the four-month ultrasound, when they'd find out the sex of the baby, Raúl and Sofía's mother, Katerine, came for support. Katerine had grown more accepting of the situation and of Ernesto's commitment to becoming a good father. They had a bet going on the sex.

"Who's going to win?" Katerine asked Raúl, trying to engage him.

"It's a boy," he said. "I'm sure of it." He went back to fiddling with his phone.

Sofía and Ernesto burst out of the door, holding the ultrasound copy. "So, who's betting what? What do you think?" Sofía said, laughing at everyone's hungry faces. Ernesto was silent, shaking slightly.

"Don't mess around!" Katerine scolded her daughter. "Just tell us!"

Sofía smiled and raised her eyebrow.

"Boy!" Katerine said.

"*Girl!*" Sofía shouted.

Ernesto shook his head, smiling, and then began to cry. Knowing the sex had somehow made everything more real.

"Girl?" said Raúl. "Wow."

Ernesto stood off to the side, breathless. He could hardly speak as they walked out of the hospital. His body felt light and feeble—he struggled to push open the door.

They walked Sofía to her mother's car.

"We won't know for *sure* until the baby comes out!" said Katerine.

They cackled.

"We're going to take the bus," Ernesto said, referring to himself and Raúl, when they got to the car. Katerine shrugged. He gave Sofía a kiss goodbye and rubbed her stomach.

The twins stared into the distance, waiting for the bus. They had nothing to say, and that was fine. Here on the sidewalk, no one knew them, no one wanted to smash their heads in with rocks, no one loved them—people just passed them by. And though there was something forlorn about Oakland's sea of anonymity, being alone together, just the two of them, had a refreshing weightlessness. They soaked in the sunlight and nicotine, hoping the bus would take a little longer to come.

Ernesto shook his head and smiled in disbelief. He wanted to tell his parents but was still afraid. It would mean announcing one more financial obstacle. It would also, he felt, remind them of how separate their lives were. Now that he was starting a new family, they might never know.

Later that week he got up the guts to call home. "My girlfriend is having a baby," he said to his mother. "A baby girl."

"Oh," Esperanza said. She began to cry, then collected herself.

"Just make sure you bring the baby home someday so I can meet her," she said.

"Okay," he promised. "I will."

• • •

Sometimes there was no rain in El Salvador; sometimes the rain came at the wrong time. The land was thirsty. All over the country, the cattle were dying, and the corn was drying up on the vine. In April 2016, the president of El Salvador declared a national water shortage emergency. That had never happened before. Some 3.5 million people in Central America were at risk of food insecurity or were already hungry.

Wilber Sr., the old man with thirteen children—three up north, six in El Salvador, four buried in the churchyard—sometimes went out to the land to pray.

That summer his tomato crop was bad, due to a problem he'd never seen before. The tomatoes, though they had a good enough flavor—not his best, but good—were pallid in color, their skin a mottled orange yellow. Seen from far away, they were easily mistaken for citrus. He couldn't figure out what had gone wrong. His wife took them into town, anyway, but she couldn't make the sale. "Sweet flavor, good price!" she crooned to the crowds of the roadside market. But who wanted to buy the wrong-color fruit?

Then there was the dust. A dust cloud from the Sahara, as he understood it, had flown in and settled onto his crops. Who knew what damage it might be doing to the soil? And last year there had been the problem with the coffee—rust, they called it. Every crop had its own plague.

Wilber Sr. was still feeble from sickness, from age. His sons weren't helping much anymore, so he was mostly on his own out there in the sun, harvesting the forlorn tomatoes. He hadn't been a perfect father, a perfect husband, but he'd tried.

A thought came to him, as it often did after prayer: beets.

"I came up with an idea," he announced to his family—the members who remained—that evening. "The tomatoes don't have the right color, and they aren't sweet enough. So my solution is as follows. You know that in some places they use beets to make sugar? Yes, exactly. Well"—he paused—"my plan is to grow beets, take the juice from the beets, and pour the juice at the base of the tomato plants."

That way, he reasoned, the roots would suck up the deep dark color as well as the sweet flavor. Either it would bring life back to the farm, or it would work otherwise. Whatever God's will.

A person could slip out of this world so easily. But this project with the beets made him want to stay at least a little longer. Every plan was a Hail Mary for the faithful, after all. Even if the rain never came again, even if he was forced to sell his land, his inheritance, Wilber Sr. would work until he no longer could.

After learning that Ernesto was having a kid, Maricela couldn't sleep. She'd dreamed of having a niece for her daughters to play with. How nice, to be an aunt, to no longer be the only one of the nine with a kid. But Ernesto? Why not Wilber or Ricardo—the ones who were actually ready, or at least older? She'd heard the girl was younger, that poor thing. She knew what it would be like for her. Girls had so few options. She knew her brother was a good guy, but guys, like Cesar, couldn't be trusted to stick around. And being good to the girl almost certainly meant leaving his own family behind. Her brother had set roots in the United States: his phones, his sneakers, his clothes, his education, and now his baby.

A few weeks later Maricela woke up to a hard kick into her stomach. It nearly knocked the wind out of her. Ricardo.

"What the fuck were you thinking?" he said, practically spitting. She had forgotten to turn the light off in the house's main room. She could smell the liquor on him, and he was swaying. "Stupid bitch." He left the room.

The baby was now crying. Maricela hushed her and lay still until she was sure that Ricardo had fallen asleep.

He came home drunk again a few nights later, but this time he confided in her. "They want me to join," he said. Meaning the gangs. "But they told me I'd have to kill Dad."

Maricela was too stunned to respond.

"And I don't have the courage to do that."

It was a rare moment of closeness, this confiding, and it didn't last. Ricardo pinned everything on her, it seemed, from the family's financial circumstances to his own lack of options in life. After that night he grew even more vitriolic, as if he were punishing her for knowing his secrets.

She told Ernesto and Raúl over Facebook, "Ricardo's out of control." She couldn't tell their father, because he'd confront Ricardo, and then Ricardo would find another way to punish her. She stayed fearfully quiet, avoided eye contact, and whisked the kids away from sight. She tried to become invisible in her own house.

• • •

Then in August, after more than three years, Sebastian's brother was released from a jail sentence for his affiliation with Barrio 18 and came back to La Colonia. Rumors went that he was hunting down people all over the region—rival gang members who he thought had snitched on him or had something to do with why he ended up in jail.

Maricela knew nothing of this until Ricardo came home one night and pulled her into a room. She stiffened, expecting another beating.

"Don't go outside," he said. Someone had passed word to him that, to avenge the deaths of the people Sebastian's brother had killed, the local MS-13 guys were looking to kill not just Sebastian's brother but other members of his family. Sebastian lived in Houston now, so they couldn't get to him.

"They want to kill you and Lupita," he said.

"Lupita?"

The three-year-old was, after all, part of Sebastian's bloodline. "Don't go outside," Ricardo repeated. That was all he had to offer, and he did so with a gruff tenderness, despite all that had passed between them. She believed he was telling the truth or, anyway, what he knew of the truth. As always, who knew what word on the street was real and what was misinformation?

She stayed inside with her daughters for a few days. She couldn't call the police about the threats—one never knew whom they were working for. Finally she risked taking the bus to go talk to Cesar.

In his tiny place in town, she told him what happened.

"I think the only thing I can do is go north," she said. Cesar barely earned enough now to cover his rent, much less pay her way, but she thought her brothers would be willing to help.

Later, she called Sebastian to tell him what was going on. He hadn't been in touch with his brother, he said, but he believed her.

"I can pay for Lupita," he concluded, "but not for you."

To get them to Mexico would cost three thousand dollars each, and she'd have to pay her share of that, then figure out some way to cross the border. A *coyote* would charge her at least eight thousand dollars for the full trip, start to finish. She knew that if she went, she could only take one of her daughters, and it would have to be Lupita. She'd leave Leiny behind—at least for now.

Sending Lupita alone was out of the question. It could put her in even more danger, and even if she crossed safely, Maricela might never see her again. And who would take care of her up there—her absentee father in Houston? Her preoccupied uncles in California? The alternative, though, was to let her stay here with a revenge bounty on her head.

At home, locked in the dark quiet of the house, she saw Trump on TV. People were saying he wouldn't win, and her family wanted to believe that was true. This man, she understood, was one more obstacle to her escape plan.

"They want to kill me and Lupita," she wrote Ernesto and Raúl. "I have to leave."

CHAPTER 19

When the twins got Maricela's messages, they panicked and called Wilber. The three of them had a family conference.

If the gangs really were after Maricela and Lupita, she needed to get out of town fast. She couldn't hide out in the house forever, and if they wanted to kill her that bad, they could always break in. But the Flores brothers simply didn't have the money to pay for her trip, let alone to support her while she got on her feet here. They knew firsthand how bad the trip was for boys; for a young woman and a little kid, they could only imagine. Plus, their parents needed her at home.

"But if they really want to kill her?" they wondered aloud.

"They told Ricardo that if he joins, he has to kill Dad," Raúl said.

Wilber had seen pictures of Ricardo on Facebook looking bloated from drinking.

"If he does anything to Dad, I'll fly down there myself and kill him," Ernesto said, his face reddening.

How had it all come to this?

Maricela messaged her brothers daily. She had heard a rumor circulating through Central America that children and parents with young kids who crossed the United States border were being offered *permisos,* permission papers to stay in the United States, if they turned themselves in. There were no *permisos,* as her brothers had told her again and again. Best case, she would be in detention for a few weeks and then be allowed to await court in Oakland, likely with an ankle bracelet.

Maricela, simultaneously driven by fear and starry-eyed at the prospect of finally going north, could not be dissuaded. And she became obsessed with the deadline the *coyotes* had given her: November 2016.

The boys certainly couldn't put several thousand dollars together within a month. What was the urgency with November? they asked.

"Because then it will be the elections," she finally explained. Never mind that even if Trump was elected, none of his policies would be enacted until the new year after inauguration. Yet the rumor stuck like truth: more walls, no *permisos,* no chance to start anew.

"It's very unlikely he will win," I told Raúl one day at school during lunchtime, as he slumped on the couch outside my office, ruminating over what to do.

"He's going to win," Raúl said. "I know it."

I told him he was always thinking the worst would happen.

"Maybe so, but I know he's going to win." He shook his head. "People love him. And then all the Latinos are going home." He would always be, he felt, an outsider.

In mid-October, Ernesto was sleeping over at Sofía's house when she woke up in pain. Within a few minutes her water had broken and they loaded into her mother's car for the hospital. She labored for around ten hours, writhing with each contraction. Ernesto pressed into her back, as they had been taught at the parenting and birthing classes they'd attended. But with each contraction, she seemed to lose a little strength. "I can't," she said, sweating and shaking her head. "I can't do it."

"Echale ganas," he encouraged. "Don't worry, just keep trying, you've got this."

"The baby's coming," he texted Raúl between contractions.

"My baby is on its way," he wrote Maricela, casting a virtual net across the city, the continent, to feel closer to his family.

Soon enough, here was his and Sofía's daughter, alive and in the world. Her name was Isabella.

As Ernesto held his daughter for the first time, he was overcome with the realness of her, the delicate little body in his arms. He gingerly handed the baby back to Sofía and called Raúl to tell him the news.

Raúl took the bus to the hospital. Ernesto passed the baby cautiously, like a bowl filled with water, to his twin.

Raúl took her in his arms comfortably. As he stared into his niece's eyes, his face softened into an old expression—something like innocence or wonder. Raúl rocked her gently. He was totally in love.

"She had the baby. It's a girl. She is happy and healthy and doing okay," he wrote Maricela.

Ernesto took a week off from work—a week without pay—to spend time with Sofía and Isabella. Sofía, according to tradition, was to spend forty days indoors recuperating. She plugged her ears with cotton balls to keep out any outside air and adhered to a strict diet. That first week the baby slept well enough. Ernesto liked playing with her tiny hands, finger by finger, those miniature copies of his own.

Each morning before work, he stopped in and sat on the couch, where Sofía passed him the baby. Some cartoon was often on the TV. It was sad when Isabella spent his whole visit sleeping—he got only so much time with her, after all.

He held his daughter awkwardly, as new dads often do. Raúl, though, was an instant natural. Some mornings he came along and patiently waited for his turn with Isabella. She settled easily into his arms, and he walked around the room, then sat in a chair facing the corner, rocking the warm, sleeping bundle.

"Let me have her," Ernesto said as a Spanish *Finding Nemo* blared from the screen in front of them. It was almost time to go. Raúl shrugged and gave her back. Across the room on the other couch, Sofía snuggled against Ernesto's shoulder, peeking at the baby. They turned their eyes to the TV, watching raptly, laughing uproariously.

Ernesto checked his phone, careful not to rock his daughter. Time to go. He handed the baby to Sofía, kissed her on the forehead, and reluctantly walked out the door.

Ernesto had started the school year taking classes in Alameda, but by Isabella's birth, he had quit. He'd go back later, he felt—now was the time for another job. Sofía had started taking classes at the school for teen moms before Isabella was born, and she'd return there in January.

Raúl enrolled in the twelfth grade at Oakland International. He wanted to go to school; he needed to—"for my future," he said—but sometimes he just couldn't pull himself out of bed. Staying in school kept him from getting another job, but he wasn't going often enough to actually earn the credits he needed to move toward his goal of graduating, let alone become fluent in English. He'd take on the whole weight of the family debt, but he wanted to maintain some sliver of hope for a better future for himself.

He sent $750 home to keep the lenders at bay.

"They're going to sell it," Maricela said.

"I'll send more," Raúl promised.

The lenders were making calls to find buyers for the land now. Raúl really was the only hope to stave them off.

"I'll suffer if it means saving them," he said. He was deadly serious. For two months he ate little, bought nothing, paid his rent, and sent money home. He knew well enough that his full-blown effort was late; he thought of all the money he'd wasted on clothes, on booze. Still, he tried. Every time he sent money was a triumph.

But the money barely made a dent. And now it wasn't just the land; Maricela needed his help, too—her life, if the rumors were true, depended on it.

But it was no use. In time, the numbers, and his growling stomach, became a paralytic. The hole was just too deep. He called his mother in La Colonia one day, in broken sobs. "I can't, I can't do it alone," he whimpered. He explained his depression, his anxiety, and how, because of the baby, Ernesto couldn't help for now. Raúl wasn't sleeping, always had the jitters. "I'm afraid I'm going crazy," he told her.

"Don't worry," Esperanza said. "Take care of yourself." He mustn't let the stress kill him, she told him—she needed him safe and well. The debt was too much for all of them. They'd sell one parcel of their land to save the other and get out from under the creditors for good.

Raúl felt a mix of shame and relief.

"Thank you," he said. "I'm sorry." He felt the urge to crawl into a quiet place and stay there for a while. But one can't just withdraw from the world, Raúl knew—he'd tried that before, until love and duty had beckoned him back. Independence didn't mean doing everything by himself; being his own man didn't mean being alone. He needed the rest of them. Even Ernesto. Him, most of all.

After the phone call, Esperanza told Wilber Sr. and Maricela that it was over. There was no more debt, she said. It was driving Raúl crazy. They had to accept that the land was lost, the debt too high for them to ever climb their way out.

Wilber and Maricela protested, but Esperanza held her ground. She was determined. "Enough."

Wilber and Maricela sat down to do the math. If they sold one plot of land, valued now at around forty thousand dollars, they thought, they could pay off the debt, keep the other plot, and still have some money.

It pained Wilber to sell the land, which meant so much more than money. But it had to be done. "What's done is done," he told Maricela. But he didn't want to talk to his sons for a while. Esperanza didn't hold it against them.

"We're fine, everything's fine," Esperanza told Raúl. "We'll sell the land and have more money. We'll be okay!" Raúl knew she was lying, but all the same he felt somehow lighter. No more debt. Now, like Ernesto, he was free to start from scratch.

He broke the news to his brother gently: they were selling the land. No need to rub it in, to make him feel at fault. Ernesto sighed, then began to cry. He took it harder than Raúl had expected. He did care.

When Raúl thought back to Guatemala now, or his enemies back home, he realized he no longer felt nauseated. The terror and the rage had faded. But this came at a price: he was also forgetting. The contours of his past were blurring, and even his mother's face now took time to focus against the screen of memory. The thing about growing up and moving on was that you also had to let some good things go.

He asked a friend to give him a tattoo: two black feathers on the inside of his forearm, alongside the word *Dream*.

In El Salvador a tattoo would have been seen as the mark of a gangster. Here it could mean anything. The new tattoo covered up his scars.

The main parcel of the Flores family land, their *herencia,* went up for sale.

One month and a day after Isabella was born, it was Election Day.

As the news came in of Trump's potential upset victory, the guys who worked the kitchen in the sushi restaurant began shouting and swearing.

"Jesus Christ," one said.

"Pack your bags, boys—that's it," said another.

"Fucking racists."

Ernesto listened, head hung.

As they shut down the restaurant for the night, the owners, a Japanese family, seemed distraught. "There will be war," they said. "This man is going to cause many wars."

On November 9, 2016, the whole world seemed surprised by the election outcome, but not the Flores siblings. They always did prepare for the worst, even as they hoped for much, much more.

They talked to Wilber. The election had shaken him deeply. Trump threatened to purge the country of undocumented people—to deport two million, probably three million, people. After nearly a decade in the United States without papers, deportation seemed likelier than ever before and his future, in certain ways, all the more precarious. Who knew what tomorrow held for him?

220

He decided to make some changes.

Wilber called Raúl to let him know that he and Gabby had broken up for good. They had had too many fights, with too much stress.

Now Wilber had an idea. "I want to find an apartment for all three of us," he said. It bothered him that his brothers lived in a crappy room in a house where they couldn't use the kitchen or leave their shampoo in the shower or leave their door unlocked. Maybe, he thought, the three of them could make a real home together.

This way, too, Maricela would have a place to crash if she did come north.

Time, the election, and the troubles back home were a uniting force. They started looking for apartments together, the three Flores men. Maybe Maricela would join them, maybe not. The specter of violence down south, the specter of deportation up north: their worlds were determined by it all.

At least Isabella was a citizen. They worried about her growing up in a place rife with racism, having fewer opportunities, being hated or scorned. But Isabella was also a clean slate—a chance for her family, and her world, to raise someone right. She'd inherit the earth, a full Salvadoran American. More than that, she'd make it better.

As to how the racism and fear in the political landscape would settle, "all we can do is wait," said Raúl. Ernesto agreed.

All along, things had happened to them—the desert trip, the murder, the kidnapping, their country's unraveling, and now Ernesto's fatherhood—that were beyond reason. They knew they'd been dealt a terrible lot but had also had some unbelievable strokes of luck. To be so very lucky and so terribly unlucky could disorient a person; you never knew where the next punch might come from, or if it would come at all.

Maricela sent them a message. Their cousin Juan was now the local MS-13 boss.

Early one morning in December in La Colonia, the Floreses heard shots from down the road. A farmer in his seventies, just a little older than Wilber Sr., had been executed by the side of the road. He died instantly, shot through the head and the chest. The police, they found out later, suspected Barrio 18. No one in the community would talk to the police or the press, except on condition of anonymity.

When Maricela heard the shots, she thought at first they were meant for her. The whole family stayed inside for a few days.

It rattled everyone—in La Colonia and in Oakland—that the shooting had happened so close to their home and in broad daylight. The twins could picture right where the man had been gunned down.

The following week Maricela picked up the phone, curious about an unknown number that was calling.

"Listen, girl," the voice said. "You're going to pay us five hundred dollars, or we're going to kill you."

As with many threats in El Salvador, it was hard to know whether the call was coming from real gangsters. But it felt real to her, compounding the threats that already existed. Regardless of whether they were linked to Sebastian's brother, or whether the gangs really had her address, she wanted out of town.

She went and stayed with Cesar for a while and took the two girls with her, nervous on the bus lest someone followed her. There, she stayed inside while Cesar went to work.

She heard from her father that someone had agreed to buy the smaller parcel of land. "Thirty thousand dollars," he told her. Enough to pay off the debt—now around twenty-four thousand dollars—and have some left over. They'd been hoping for more, but after so few bites, this was good news.

There was a catch.

"The man lives in the United States," Wilber Sr. explained. "He will pay off the land little by little." They'd still be relying on small monthly installments from the States, which they'd use to pay off their own debt over time. They took the deal. At least they still had their larger parcel of land. As long as they could farm it, they wouldn't starve.

During this time her sisters, Marina and Lucia, had each joined a convent. It was the safest bet for both of them, to be protected and cared for. Maricela was the only sister left at home, living with Ricardo, the drunk who flirted with the gangs, and her two little brothers. No one to help her with the babies now, no one to talk to—her friends, her closest siblings, all gone.

If only they'd sent her to the North instead of her brothers. For now, Maricela wasn't leaving, but she hadn't given up hope. If she didn't go, she knew she'd spend her whole life wondering what might have been. If she did go, she'd likely always wonder, as her brothers did, whether she'd made the right decision—whether, in fact, she'd had the option to stay.

For now, Cesar loved her and, more important, valued her. But she knew that she also had to find value for herself—especially in this world where women were still, so often, second class. She was determined to forge a life distinct from the one she had inherited from her parents' circumstances. She wanted Lupita and Leiny to find more than she had to give them, and to do that, she'd have to start them off better than where she'd begun. Here or there she would manage to improve the hand she'd been dealt; she and her girls in her wake would—quietly, maybe, but unflinchingly—carry on. What other choice was there?

The twins decided to take a bike ride up into the Oakland hills. They tore along a paved path that skirted the ridge from Inspiration Point, feeling their wheels catch air over the speed bumps. From up here they could see San Francisco and, beyond it, the ocean: the Pacific, the same ocean they'd seen as kids during the annual trip for good students in La Colonia. The dry and blistered hillsides reminded them of Texas, a time that felt further and further away. Ernesto took a photo and posted it.

Up here, above the lives they had built, and the country they had built them in, the brothers cruised over a cattle grate, past barbed-wire fences. Fences, walls, deserts, oceans. People got what they needed to survive or died trying. So far they'd made it.

"*¡Animal!*" Raúl shouted. "Bitch, I'll kick your ass!"

It occurred to the Flores twins that there would likely never again be a time when their entire nuclear family, all eleven of them, were back together. Things had changed forever. Nearly half the family land was gone, too, a fact that pained them, along with other wounds. At the same time there was a bright side: the debt was canceled. This moment offered the sense of a real beginning. Raúl would get to school on time, and next semester, Ernesto would re-enroll in the community college classes to get his certificate of completion. He wanted to set a good example for his daughter, after all. This month, they were sure, they could send some money home to help their family—pure help, not just a piddle toward an unbeatable debt. If they saved enough, their father could buy another parcel of land he'd found for sale—a small one, but a fertile one; better, even, than the one they'd lost. They were getting another chance, and they'd do it right this time.

They dipped and soared in the parched folds of California, whooping and hollering like kids, until it was time to pack up the bikes and head back down to the flats, to work. Back at Inspiration Point, they looked out over the frenetic plane of Oakland, the shimmering bay, and across to the Golden Gate.

From up high, just the two of them, they could hold on to that notion of possibility. This, they supposed, was the irresistible tug of the American Dream. For a sunny instant they were pulled in.

AFTERWORD

"Me tiraron," one of my students told me when I first started working at Oakland International. "They threw me." At that point my Spanish wasn't great, so I thought I'd misheard. He explained, "They put me in a bag, and when the guards weren't looking, they threw me over the fence." *Me tiraron.* His smugglers, holding on to each end of the sack, had tossed my sixteen-year-old student over the twelve-foot wall. The boy undid himself from the sack and took off running. He wasn't caught. Wall or no wall, he would have done anything, he told me, to get to the United States.

My thirteen years of experience working with, interviewing, and reporting alongside thousands of refugees and migrants like the Flores twins have shown me that few people actually *want* to leave their homes. People most often leave because staying has become unbearable, even impossible.

Global poverty is a massive driver of migration to the United States and around the globe. Who among us wouldn't flee economic collapses, droughts or famine in order to feed ourselves, to feed our families? But as the story of the Flores brothers reveals, along with the stories of others they and I met during this journey, today's unauthorized migration across our southern border is driven largely—though of course not entirely—by violence.

Since the change in administration and the initial publication of this book, MS-13 has become all but a household name in the United States. President Trump has said that MS-13 members "have transformed beautiful quiet neighborhoods into bloodstained killing fields" and blames the influx of Central Americans, like the Flores twins—many of whom are themselves fleeing MS-13's violence and threats back home. In addition to criminalizing the new young immigrants, the Trump administration's repeated invocation of MS-13 only helps boost the gang's tough image, and thus its power.

Another result of Donald Trump's anti-immigrant rhetoric is that undocumented immigrants like Wilber feel on shakier ground than ever before. And they are. Since Mr. Trump took office, arrests and deportations of immigrants in the United States have increased, and a ban on new entrants from certain Muslim countries has been put into place. The Trump administration has separated thousands of immigrant children, and even some infants, from their parents in order to send the message that unauthorized immigration to the United States will be met with unspeakable cruelty. The current administration also threatens to penalize sanctuary cities, like Oakland—places where local law enforcement opt not to collaborate with immigration authorities in turning over potential undocumented immigrants. It is also expanding detention facilities for both children and adults.

Though the United States has created alternatives to detention programs for unaccompanied minors, conditions in the short-term *hieleras* are often unconscionable, and allegations of abuse persist within ORR-contracted facilities like the one in which the Flores twins were housed.

Appalling conditions in adult detention centers continue, too, particularly in those housing families—malnourished children, scabies and lice outbreaks, sexual abuse, limited access to health care, and cramped quarters. In August 2016, after decades of public pressure and numerous press exposés of negligence and mismanagement in private prisons, the US Department of Justice announced that it would no longer outsource incarceration in the criminal justice system to private contractors, though private contracts for immigration detention facilities remain the same. Trump's administration reversed the plans to end private detention contracts for criminal incarceration, and in one of his early executive orders, President Trump instructed US Immigration and Customs Enforcement (ICE) to begin immediately constructing *more* facilities and initiating new contracts. Stocks in companies like the Corrections Corporation of America and the Geo Group—companies that also run immigration facilities—have soared since he was elected. Private corporations continue to profit off the adult immigration detention system; the more migrants put into detention centers, the more money corporations make. This is a significant, and sinister, motivating factor in the Trump administration's plans to expand immigration facilities.

In 2016, ICE processed 352,882 new immigrant detainees and, along with Customs and Border Protection, deported over 450,000 people. In 2015 a total of 21,920 were deported to El Salvador—9 percent of total removals. The Obama administration deported more than 2.5 million people from the United States—more than any administration to date. Toward the end of his tenure, the number of deportations declined.

President Trump campaigned on an immigration hardline, and in his first one hundred days alone, his team issued executive orders and guidelines to ramp up immigration enforcement, increase expedited removals at the border (where newly arrived immigrants would be deported without first seeing a judge), and deport people with minor offenses, like driving without a license, on their record, or even those merely charged with a crime. Less than a month after the inauguration, an internal Department of Homeland Security memo also issued new guidelines saying that parents who paid a *coyote* to bring their children north could be subject to prosecution for facilitating smuggling. The following year, the administration would begin, as a matter of standard policy, separating children from their parents at the border and locking them up.

The exact nature of future immigration enforcement remains unknown. But the resulting climate, one of fear and uncertainty, with hate crimes against immigrants dramatically on the rise, is not something we have to accept. Much can be done to improve our policies and systems for assisting immigrants with paperwork and legal counsel, as well as the more than eleven million undocumented immigrants already living here, the tens of thousands in immigration detention at any given time, and the hundreds crossing the border every day.

The data clearly shows that access to legal counsel significantly determines the outcome of a child's ability to gain protection according to the law. Expecting children to represent themselves in court—in such a high-stakes situation that could significantly impact their well-being (and in some cases their very lives)—is unethical.

In many ways, schools like Oakland International are on the front lines of immigration. Across the United States, English-language learners are twice as likely to drop out of high school as those fluent in English—and these statistics are even more dire for students newly arrived to the country.

As low-skilled jobs dwindle, far fewer careers are possible without a high school diploma. The link between dropping out of school and incarceration is noticeable: though nine out of ten adults in the United States have a high school diploma or equivalent, 69 percent of inmates in federal and local jails did not complete high school. A study by the Alliance for Excellent Education claims it costs $12,643 to educate a student for a year and costs more than twice as much—$28,323—to house someone for a year in prison. The study also posits that reducing US dropout rates by just 5 percent would lead to $18.5 billion in annual government crime savings and would increase national earnings by $1.2 billion. Education, particularly for newly arrived immigrants, who lack many or any connections to the larger community, can, when done right, provide a sense of community, belonging, and purpose. We have seen all over the world, and throughout history, that when young people feel excluded from society they seek belonging in its fringes, among its shadows. This could very easily have happened to the twins.

Related policy shifts would be important steps in ensuring the justice and humanity of the US immigration system. But even more critical problems affecting immigration must be addressed outside our borders.

Many politicians, including President Trump, have made border protection a central issue, the notion being that securing the border would make immigration go away. Though immigration enforcement walls are now being built all over the world, from Hungary to Norway to Thailand, the fact is that walls do not secure borders; they simply make them more complicated to cross. Hundreds of thousands of undocumented migrants cross US borders every year, undeterred by the threat of death. Nor are they deterred by the 650 miles of wall that already exist. That's how bad the circumstances they're leaving are.

Threats of a wall. Racism. An America-first mind-set. This kind of exclusionist policy ignores the legacy of US responsibility for the Central American catastrophe. A war is raging to our south, though we seem to refuse to call it one, and American policy is what fueled the wars that preceded it. We supplied guns to and trained armies and death squads who ended up perpetrating scorched-earth massacres during the Salvadoran Civil War; bodies are still being exhumed and identified today, over three decades later. We created free-trade deals that not only negatively impacted Americans but also gutted the earnings of small-scale farmers south of the Mexican border. Transnational corporations like Chiquita, Dole, and Del Monte bought up land and cornered the export markets for local medium- and small-scale businesses, making it more difficult for rural families (like the Floreses) to earn a living.

Economic despair has vexed El Salvador for decades. There are ways to create alternatives to the Northern Triangle's gang economy, though. Investing in education is a significant one. So is investing in infrastructure to create jobs in local markets, in products made "at home." The United States cannot at once be isolationist—build a wall to keep others out, kill the trade deals with other countries—*and* global, selectively enjoying the benefits of an international economy, like lower-cost imports, a cut-rate outsourced workforce, and cheap labor in our fields here at home. We have played a major part in creating the violence in Central America, and we must play a major part in solving it.

This argument is more than moral: it is also pragmatic. If every kid could go to school and get a job in Central America, they would have less incentive to join a gang or to leave home. But this scenario cannot become a reality without deep international investment—not just in projects but in whole systems: education, health, economic infrastructure, community policing. Recent successes in peaceably ending internal unrest—in northern Uganda, South Africa, Rwanda, and even the Central American civil wars—can provide guidance on disarming conflict and reconciliation. Disbanding the gangs would require providing a real, systemic alternative, and the United States must play a part.

People migrate now for the same reason they always have: survival. The United States can build a wall, dig a two-thousand-mile trench, patrol with drones and military-grade vehicles and machine guns, and put thousands more guards at the border. Desperate migrants will still find another way. They'll take to the sea, they'll stuff themselves into bags, they'll dig tunnels, they'll push into rougher and rougher territory. They'll send their children alone.

Plenty of work must be done here in the United States to achieve responsible immigration reform—but to focus only on *our* side of the border is to miss the urgent and persistent realities at the very heart of undocumented immigration. It is also to misunderstand the lives and motivations of the millions who have made this country their home. Immigrants to the United States were and still are determined by the places from which they came, and we in turn are determined by them. Whether by choice, by necessity, or both, they are also Americans. Just ask the Flores twins.

—Lauren Markham

ACKNOWLEDGMENTS

I owe thanks to many people who supported me during the process of dreaming about, researching, and writing this book.

Many books offered me insight and revelation, including Joan Didion's *Salvador*, Luis Alberto Urrea's *The Devil's Highway*, Ted Conover's *Coyotes*, Sonia Nazario's *Enrique's Journey*, Óscar Martínez's *The Beast* and *A History of Violence*, Mark Danner's *The Massacre at El Mozote*, Carlos Henríquez Consalvi's *Broadcasting the Civil War in El Salvador*, and Marc Zimmerman's *El Salvador at War: A Collage Epic*. *Insight Crime* and the dogged, masterful reporting of *El Faro* offered invaluable information and perspective; I owe much gratitude to their work.

I found my brilliant and loving agent, Sylvie Greenberg, at exactly the right time, when the seeds of this book had just begun to germinate. I couldn't have found a better champion or friend in this pursuit. My unparalleled editor, Meghan Houser, provided constant guidance, cheerleading, insight, and patience, and I am forever grateful to her for taking a chance on this project and for breathing life into it. My fact-checker, Sharon Riley, is a research wizard who took great pains to ensure that I'd gotten things right. Thank you to Beverly Horowitz, Audrey Ingerson, and the entire team at Delacorte Press for believing that this book should be brought to younger audiences. Thank you to Erica Moroz for her expert skills in adapting this book from its original form.

I have been blessed with the best and most supportive of teachers. Early on, there was Andy Johnston, Randy Barnett, David Loeb, Ed McCatty, and Trevor Peard. Thank you to Robert Cohen and David Bain at Middlebury College for pushing me further while cheering me on. My professors at Vermont College of Fine Arts helped me fuse craft, language, and the arc of story. Thank you, Jess Row, David Jauss, and most of all, Abby Frucht; thank you also to Mary Ruefle, Larry Sutin, and Ralph Angel, for invaluable mentorship and inspiration postgraduation ("Your job is to write the best sentences possible," Ralph reminds me, "no matter what you're writing about"). Deep gratitude to the folks from the Middlebury Fellowship, Bill McKibben, Janisse Ray, Rebecca Solnit, Chris Shaw, and Sue Kavanagh, who model the art of righteous writing and living, and who believed in my first feature story, which set me on the path to becoming a journalist. Likewise, Malia Wollan, Jack Hitt, Alan Burdick, and Michael Pollan at the UC Berkeley 11th Hour Food and Farming Fellowship provided me the generous support, community, and guidance I needed to continue to report on unaccompanied minors. Thank you.

Paul Reyes at *VQR* urged me to pitch him my very nebulous, notional story about kids who came to this country alone. That encouragement launched this book. Wes Enzinna took a chance on my second unaccompanied minors story. Each time Paul and Wes have edited my work over the years they have taught me how to be a better journalist and a better writer.

Funding from the French American Foundation and the Pulitzer Center for Crisis Reporting supported the research of key sections of this book. The Rotary Foundation provided me the time and perspective that allowed me to conceive of this project, and the Mesa Refuge offered quiet and space on the edge of California where I could hunker down and write, and also dream. Clarity for the original idea I owe to the Southern California Vipassana Center, and the desert.

Tom Verner and the North Branch School were the reason I ended up in El Salvador in the first place, years ago. Friends in El Salvador have helped me immeasurably since then: Melisa Oliva, Lucy Guzman, Vilma Ortiz, Emilia Estrada, Luis Mario, Billy, and Irma. And to the woman who dragged me up the stairs into her shop and cared for me after I passed out in the middle of Santa Tecla with a case of dehydration: thank you.

Langan Courtney, Nate Dunstan, Ariana Flores, Sylvia Townsend, and Igor Radulovich have imparted much wisdom over the years as colleagues and as friends. Jean Yamasaki and Eleni Wolf Roubiatis are incredible human beings and tireless advocates who have taught me and heartened me along the way. Katie Annand did the same, and more—thank you for being open to this project.

I knew the day I met Carmelita Reyes that I would find a home at Oakland International—even though the school didn't exist yet. Carmelita, Sailaja Suresh, Thi Bui, Liza Richheimer, and all the founding teachers, thank you for your brilliance and incarnating that world and letting me be a part of it. Thank you to the later staff, too, especially Salem Peterson, Mallory Moser, Brooke Toczylowski, Cormac Kilgallen, Raquel Franker, Michelle Rostampour, and Shahrzad Makaremi (these last three held down the fort any time I was away writing or researching this book, and I am forever grateful). The people of OIHS are the most dedicated and inspirational people I know; I love them all like brothers and sisters, and like siblings, they have enriched my life and perspective on the world. The students have done this perhaps most of all. And, Mr. David Hansen: this book might not exist if it weren't for you. Thank you for your uplifting work, for introducing me to the twins, and for always pushing my thinking forward.

Thank you to the wide circle of beloved friends who endured my anxiety and chatter as the book took shape. My porch people, my friend family: thank you for your patience and intelligence and joy. Luke Carson, Eric Skaar, and Liz and John Frankel helped me understand the issues. Thank you to the Middlebury Fellows and the UC Berkeley Food Fellows, and most especially to Heather Gilligan and Bridget Huber for helping me turn so many ideas into stories. Carrie Nazzaro, Theresa Kenney, Dani Fisher, Evan Bissell, Kendra Ing, Niko McConnie-Saad, Melissa Chou, and Anna Goldstein, as well as journalist pals Diane Jeantet, Ian Gordon, and Holly Haworth, offered love, wisdom, smarts, adventure, and fun. Thank you to Liara Tamani for unbridled positivity and inspiration; Robin MacArthur for her courage and singing prose and cross-continental good vibes; and Sierra Crane Murdoch for her grace and commitment to truth telling. (I read everything these three women write with pride and a small pang of loving envy—you should, too.)

Lindsay Whalen provided me with laughter, moral support, expert guidance, edits, and suggestions the whole way through—how I am so lucky to have a best friend who is also an editor and a brilliant writer, I'll never quite know. I can, and do, talk to Hannah Epstein from takeoff to landing on any flight, literal or metaphoric. Her love and encouragement have carried me through so many triumphs and heartaches on the page and in my life. I cannot imagine earth without these two. (Thanks, too, to the Epstein and Whalen families, and the extended Gucciardis, who have taken me in as their own.)

I am lucky to come from a loving and supportive family who, regardless of political beliefs, have loyally bolstered my pursuits while training me in the art of storytelling. Thank you to the extended Markham/Read clan, and most especially to Uncle Read for reading this book with an open heart. Thank you to my father, John Markham, for being my unwavering champion, someone committed to the notion of a vocation, and the best raconteur I know; to my mother, Liz Read, who is as selfless and supportive as they come and will accompany me on any journey near and far; and to my brother, Chris, who always pushes me to see the other side of things and can make me laugh and think.

Ben Gucciardi is the anchor of all anchors, righteous and brilliant, a man who walks to the thump of the world's heartbeat. Thank you for keeping me healthy, happy, rooted, full of wonder, and for helping me clear the path for this book.

Thank you to the entire "Flores" family for letting me into your worlds so as to be able to tell this story. And thank you, gentle readers, for making it to the end.

NOTES

Methodology

To write this book, I spent two years traveling on and off throughout the United States, Mexico, Guatemala, and El Salvador to get a glimpse of the perilous migration trail north, as well as the scope of violence in Central America. I spent countless hours with the Flores twins and their extended family in Oakland and in El Salvador, interviewing and getting to know them so I could render their very personal stories and very challenging circumstances.

I relied heavily on my professional experience working with immigrant families at Oakland International High School and at other organizations, and on my past reporting on unaccompanied minors and El Salvador for *VICE, Pacific Standard, VQR,* and the *New Republic.* All this figured into my narrative both explicitly (some scenes in this book are edited versions of stories that appeared in those magazines) and as background.

This book was written through a combination of first-hand reporting and reconstructed scenes of my reporting in

El Salvador, Mexico, Texas, and California. I was present for many of the Oakland-based scenes in this book, though I also reconstruct many scenes during which I was not present or that occurred before I met the twins. For them, I relied on repeated interviews with the people who had been present, as many of them as possible, to ensure that I had the facts straight; that a given memory was as strong as the memory could be; and that there were no discrepancies among their accounts. Where there were discrepancies, I have noted them in the text and offered whatever sense I could make of the variance. Wherever possible, I fact-checked the twins' accounts using available research and data. (I also employed the help of a professional fact checker.)

I could not interview several key people because there was no way to find them or because the interview would endanger the Flores family. For these same security reasons, I have changed the names of the "Flores" family members, the name of their town, and some of their identifying features. I have changed the names of some of the other characters as well. I have used the testimony of as many sources as possible without putting the subjects of this book in harm's way.

In my career as a journalist, vulnerable and marginalized people have let me into their lives based on my promise that I would tell their stories justly, respectfully, and carefully, if not necessarily to their liking. While reporting on migrants, gang-involved youth, destitute farmers, and others, I've pledged to tell the stories as fairly as I can without objectifying or endangering my subjects.

This book, however, posed a particular ethical question: I knew the Flores twins (and some of the other people in the book) from my capacity as a school administrator, not as a reporter. The twins were interested to learn that I had written magazine stories about young people in circumstances similar to theirs, that I'd been to Texas, where they'd been apprehended and detained, that I'd spent time in El Salvador, and that I was thinking about writing a book. They encouraged me to write a book about "kids like us" because, they felt, people needed to understand how hard things were in Central America, on the journey north, and even in Oakland. When it occurred to me that the best book I could write would be about them, I asked the twins (by then legally adults) what they thought about my telling their story—with their names and some identifying details changed. They took some time to think about it and finally agreed.

I agonized over the ethical question, discussing it with fellow writers, colleagues, editors, my bosses and co-workers at the school, the twins, and the twins' family. I finally came to the conclusion that if I could trust myself to tell their story respectfully and carefully, and if the twins accepted and encouraged the idea, it was appropriate for me to write this book. Ultimately, as nineteen-year-olds, they made the choice that yes, they wanted their story told.

Author's Note

x **their historical annual average:** Office of Refugee Resettlement, "Year in Review FY2013," acf.hhs.gov/orr/resource /office-of-refugee-resettlement-year-in-review-fy2013.

x **this story about unaccompanied minors:** Lauren Markham, "First the Fence, Then the System," *VQR*, Summer 2013.

Chapter 1

7 **MS-13, or Mara Salvatrucha:** Originally formed in Los Angeles in the 1980s, then brought back to El Salvador by deportees, MS-13 is now an international, though relatively decentralized, crime organization, operating in countries around the globe, including the United States. Since taking office, the Trump administration has focused much attention on the increasing (and increasingly visible) activities of MS-13 in the United States, particularly on Long Island. "They have transformed peaceful parks and beautiful quiet neighborhoods into bloodstained killing fields. They're animals," Trump said in a speech to Long Island law enforcement officers in July 2017. Trump and Attorney General Jeff Sessions have publicly blamed MS-13 activities on the influx of immigrants from Central America.

10 **85 percent of the atrocities:** The Commission on the Truth for El Salvador, "From Madness to Hope: The 12-year War in El Salvador," US Institute for Peace, January 26, 2001, usip.org/sites/default/files/file/ElSalvador-Report.pdf.

17 **Along with them came the gang culture:** Christine J. Wade, *Captured Peace: Elites and Peacebuilding in El Salvador* (Ohio University Press, 2016).

Chapter 2

20 **over 350,000 people:** Aaron Terrazas, "Salvadoran Immigrants in the United States," Migration Policy Institute, January 5, 2010.

21 **nearly 2 million Salvadorans resided:** Gustavo López, "Hispanics of Salvadoran Origin in the United States, 2013," Pew Research Center, September 15, 2015.

Chapter 3

31 **an average of twelve people murdered a day:** Overseas Advisory Council, "El Salvador 2012 Crime and Safety Report," US Department of State, April 7, 2012, osac.gov /pages/contentreportdetails.aspx?cid=12336; Overseas Advisory Council, "El Salvador 2013 Crime and Safety Report," US Department of State, April 11, 2013, osac.gov /pages/contentreportdetails.aspx?cid=13875.

31 **four times the number of homicides:** Christopher Ingraham, "There Are Now More Guns Than People in the United States," *Washington Post,* October 5, 2015.

32 **to 326,034 in 2012:** Office of Refugee Resettlement, "Facts and Data," US Department of Health and Human

Services, n.d., acf.hhs.gov/programs/orr/about/ucs/facts-and
-data.

33 **key gang leaders:** The 2012 gang truce is mired in controversy, and its exact terms, as well as who was driving the effort, remain unclear. Then-president Mauricio Funes publicly embraced the truce in 2012, but after it fell apart, he posited that it was carried out by civil society actors without his knowledge or permission.

Chapter 5

60 **When the notoriously violent Zeta and Gulf drug cartels parted ways in 2010:** Paul Imison, "Mexico's End-of-Year Crime Stats Paint a Mixed Picture," *Latin Correspondent,* December 30, 2015.

60 **major spike in homicides and other crime:** Christopher Wilson and Eugenio Weigend, "Plan Tamaulipas: A New Security Strategy for a Troubled State," Wilson Center, Mexico Institute, October 9, 2014, 7, wilsoncenter.org/sites /default/files/New_Security_Strategy_Tamaulipas_0.pdf.

60 *another* **war zone:** Wilson and Weigend, 8.

Chapter 6

64 **the Rio Grande:** Much of this section is reprinted and reworked from my article "First the Fence, Then the System," *VQR,* Summer 2013.

65 **tens of billions of dollars:** Glenn Kessler, "Trump's Dubious Claim That His Border Wall Would Cost $8 billion," *Washington Post,* February 11, 2016.

66 **the remains of hundreds of migrants:** US Border Patrol, "Sector Profile: Fiscal Year 2015," US Customs and Border Protection, January 12, 2016, cbp.gov/sites/default/files /documents/USBP%20Stats%20FY2015%20sector%20 profile.pdf.

Chapter 7

75 **24,668 minors:** Office of Refugee Resettlement, "Facts and Data," US Department of Health and Human Services, n.d., acf.hhs.gov/programs/orr/about/ucs/facts-and -data. Not all children apprehended by immigration authorities are transferred into ORR custody. Minors from countries with contiguous borders to the United States— Mexico and Canada—can be directly returned across the border if they do not assert that they have a fear of returning home.

77 **released to an official detention center:** Guillermo Cantor PhD, "Detained Beyond the Limit: Prolonged Confinement by US Customs and Border Protection Along the Southwest Border," American Immigration Council, August 18, 2016, americanimmigrationcouncil.org/research /prolonged-detention-us-customs-border-protection.

77 **an average of four days:** Cantor.

77 **within seventy-two hours:** Global Detention Project, "United States Immigration Detention Profile," May 2016, globaldetentionproject.org/countries/americas/united-states.

77 **In June 2014, the ACLU and other human and immigrant rights groups:** "Systemic Abuse of Unaccompanied Immigrant Children by US Customs and Border Protection," a June 11, 2014, complaint issued to the US Department of Homeland Security by the National Immigrant Justice Center, Americans for Immigrant Justice, the ACLU Border Litigation Project, the Florence Immigrant Rights and Refugee Project, and Esperanza Immigrant Rights Project.

77 **unaccompanied minors in the *hieleras*:** "Systemic Abuse of Unaccompanied Immigrant Children by US Customs and Border Protection."

77 *hieleras* **were leaked to the press:** The first leaked images of detention conditions for minors appeared in Brandon Darby, "Leaked Images Reveal Children Warehoused in Crowded US Cells, Border Patrol Overwhelmed," *Breitbart News,* June 5, 2014. The following week additional photos provided by Congressman Henry Cuellar (D-TX) appeared in Susan Carroll and David McCumber, "Photos Show Logjam of Immigrants Detained at Government Facility," *Houston Chronicle,* June 11, 2014.

80 **short-term housing of unaccompanied minors:** Administration for Children and Families, "Justification of Estimates

for Appropriation Committees, Fiscal Year 2017," US Department of Health and Human Services, 240, acf.hhs.gov/sites/default/files/olab/final_cj_2017_print.pdf.

80 **Flores Settlement:** "Flores Settlement Agreement and DHS Custody," Lutheran Immigration and Refugee Services, Women's Refugee Commission, and Kids in Need of Defense, n.d., docplayer.net/20957066-Flores-settlement-agreement-dhs-custody.html.

80 **Department of Homeland Security changed the rules:** Office of Refugee Resettlement, "Unaccompanied Children's Services," US Department of Health and Human Services, n.d., acf.hhs.gov/orr/programs/ucs.

80 **HHS budgeted $175 million:** Administration for Children and Families, "Justification of Estimates for Appropriation Committees, Fiscal Year 2017," US Department of Health and Human Services, 240, acf.hhs.gov/sites/default/files/olab/final_cj_2017_print.pdf.

80 **$373 million from 2016:** Administration for Children and Families, "Justification of Estimates for Appropriations Committees, Fiscal Year 2017," US Department of Health and Human Services, 16, acf.hhs.gov/sites/default/files/olab/final_cj_2017_print.pdf.

81 **2014 *Houston Chronicle* exposé:** Susan Carroll, "Crossing Alone: Children Fleeing to US Land in Shadowy System," *Houston Chronicle,* May 24, 2014.

81 **between two hundred and five hundred dollars per night:** Eighty percent of the budget was allocated to shelter costs. Eighty percent of the budget, divided by the total number of unaccompanied minors, divided by the average length of stay (thirty-four days) for that year, amounts to two hundred to five hundred dollars per night.

81 **made $659,000:** According to the 1099 forms from Southwest Key.

Chapter 8

88 **rose steadily from around 3.5 million:** "Unauthorized Immigrant Population Trends for States, Birth Countries and Regions," Pew Research Center, November 3, 2016.

88 **that number spiked to 1.7 million:** "US Unauthorized Immigration Population Estimates, Pew Research Center, November 3, 2016.

89 **the undocumented paid $11.8 billion:** "The Facts About the Individual Tax Identification Number," American Immigration Council, April 5, 2016.

89 **perhaps he could get papers:** If an undocumented immigrant marries a US citizen, he or she is indeed able to acquire citizenship but is required to leave the country for a minimum of ten years before that occurs.

96 **English-language learners:** Oakland Unified School District, ousd.org/Page/12187.

102 **"sanctuary city":** Matthew Green and Jessica Tarlton, "What Are Sanctuary Cities and How Are They Bracing for Trump's Immigration Crackdown?" KQED, February 7, 2017.

103 ***notarios,* who promised help:** Attorney General's Office, "Attorney General Submits Bill to Fight Notario Fraud, Government of the District of Columbia," DC.gov, April 29, 2016, oag.dc.gov/release/attorney-general-submits -bill-fight-notario-fraud.

103 **a child without a lawyer:** "Advocacy Factsheet," Kids in Need of Defense, November 3, 2016, supportkind.org /wp-content/uploads/2016/11/Advocacy-KIND-Fact-Sheet -Nov-2016.pdf.

103 **Legal Services for Children (LSC):** At the time, LSC was the only agency specifically dedicated to supporting unaccompanied minors in the Bay Area, and very few other agencies were taking these cases. But before the end of the year, this would change. In response to the 2014 immigration crisis and media attention, the City of Oakland, along with several local philanthropic organizations, stepped up funding to provide free legal services to these young people. By the fall of 2014, Centro Legal de la Raza and East Bay Sanctuary Covenant had hired new attorneys and prioritized these cases, taking on the lion's share (along with several other smaller organizations and LSC) of unaccompanied minors living in Oakland.

105 **victims of a violent crime:** Citizenship and Immigration Services, "Victims of Criminal Activity: U Nonimmigrant Status," US Department of Homeland Security, n.d., uscis .gov/humanitarian/victims-human-trafficking-other-crimes /victims-criminal-activity-u-nonimmigrant-status/victims -criminal-activity-u-nonimmigrant-status.

Chapter 10

112 **The paralegal recommended:** "Amy Allen" is a pseudonym.

118 **if we missed their eighteenth birthday:** At the federal level, Special Immigrant Juvenile Status (SIJS) can be granted up until the age of twenty-one, but in California, until October 2015, the finding had to be done before one's eighteenth birthday. On October 9, 2015, California governor Jerry Brown signed into law AB-900, which allowed California courts to recommend SIJS for youth between eighteen and twenty-one: "Given the recent influx of unaccompanied immigrant children arriving to the United States, many of whom have been released to family members and other adults in California and have experienced parental abuse, neglect, or abandonment, it is necessary to provide an avenue for these unaccompanied children to petition the probate courts to have a guardian of the person appointed beyond reaching 18 years of age." California Assembly, Bill 900, Chapter 694, approved October 9, 2015, leginfo.legislature.ca.gov/faces/billNavClient.xhtml?bill_id =201520160AB900.

Chapter 11

121 **get their green cards:** "Chapter 4: Special Immigrant Juvenile Status (SIJS)," Kids in Need of Defense (KIND), n.d., supportkind.org/wp-content/uploads/2015/04/Chapter-4 -Special-Immigrant-Juvenile-Status-SIJS.pdf.

128 **Berkeley's lush fruit trees:** Because the twins were going to Alameda County probate court, the courthouse was in Berkeley rather than Oakland.

Chapter 12

141 **In May 2014 alone, authorities caught more than nine thousand:** US Customs and Border Protection, "Southwest Border Unaccompanied Alien Children FY 2014," US Department of Homeland Security, updated November 24, 2015, cbp.gov/newsroom/stats/southwest-border -unaccompanied-children/fy-2014.

141 **That made forty-seven thousand since October 2013:** US Customs and Border Protection, "An Open Letter to Parents of Children Crossing Our Southwest Border," US Department of Homeland Security, June 23, 2014, dhs.gov /news/2014/06/23/open-letter-parents-children-crossing -our-southwest-border.

142 **the Women's Refugee Commission:** Sonia Nazario, "The Children of the Drug Wars: A Refugee Crisis, Not an Immigration Crisis," *New York Times,* July 11, 2014.

143 **In June the Federal Emergency Management Agency:** Much of the reporting and writing in this section comes from Lauren Markham, "FEMA Wants to House Migrant Children in Empty Big Box Stores," *New Republic,* July 20, 2014.

143 **more than $156 million in government grants:** This information comes from the Southwest Key 1099 forms.

144 **rakes in $140 million per year since 2012:** "Detention Map and Statistics," End Isolation, n.d., freedomfor immigrants.org/detention-statistics/.

144 **a cut rate of $94.95 per immigrant:** From the service agreement (contract) between the US Department of Homeland Security, Immigration and Customs Enforcement, and the Geo Group, provided to Human Rights Watch on April 29, 2015, following a Freedom of Information Act request.

Chapter 15

166 **In just June and July, more than one hundred million:** "Drought Causes $100 Million in Crop Losses in El Salvador," Phys.org, August 10, 2015, phys.org/news/2015-08 -drought-million-crop-losses-el.html.

167 **a forced bus strike:** "El Salvador Bus Drivers Strike as Gang Violence Surges," Reuters, July 27, 2015.

168 *El Diario de Hoy* reported: Pedro Carlos Mancia, Patricia Garcia, and Evelyn Chacon, "Comercios pierden $60 millones por boicot al transporte," *El Diario de Hoy,* July 30, 2015.

168 "The criminals want to hold talks": "Sánchez Cerén ofrece militarizar las unidades de transporte," *La Página,* August 9, 2015, lapagina.com.sv/nacionales/109213/2015 /08/09/Sanchez-Ceren-garantiza-seguridad-en-transporte -ante-rumores-de-nuevo-paro.

172 harsher prison sentences: Arron Daugherty, "El Salvador Supreme Court Labels Street Gangs Terrorist Groups," *Insight Crime,* August 26, 2015, insightcrime.org/news -briefs/el-salvador-supreme-court-labels-street-gangs-as -terrorist-groups.

172–173 agrupación ilícita, or illicit congregation: Decreto #459, Asamblea Legislativa, Republica de El Salvador.

173 an estimated $756 million in *renta*: "The Gangs That Cost 16% of GDP," *Economist,* May 21, 2016.

173 the sheer number of gang members: "The Gangs That Cost 16% of GDP."

174 even years awaiting trial: Institute for Criminal Policy Research, "World Prison Brief: El Salvador," prisonstudies .org/country/el-salvador.

Chapter 16

182 **in the world:** Julio Jacobo Waiselfisz, "Mapa da Violência 2015: Homicídio de Mulheres No Brasil," FLASCO Brasil, 2015, mapadaviolencia.org.br/pdf2015/MapaViolencia_2015_mulheres.pdf.

182 **a 2015 study by the United Nations Population Fund:** "Mapa de Embarazos en niñas y adolescentes en El Salvador 2015," United Nations Population Fund (UNFPA) El Salvador, July 2016, inclusionsocial.gob.sv/wp-content/uploads/2016/09/El-Salvador-Mapa-de-Embarazos-2015.pdf.

183 **jailed for even having a miscarriage:** UNICEF, "At a Glance: El Salvador, Statistics," n.d., unicef.org/infobycountry/elsalvador_statistics.html. For more details on women being jailed for miscarriage, see Rachel Nolan, "Innocents: Where Pregnant Women Have More to Fear than Zika," *Harper's,* October 2016.

183 **out of school and without a job:** "El Salvador: Education," USAID, updated November 7, 2016, usaid.gov/el-salvador/education.

183 **six out of ten:** "Invisible Victims: Migrants on the Move in Mexico," Amnesty International, April 28, 2010, amnestyusa.org/reports/invisible-victims-migrants-on-the-move-in-mexico/.

183 **even higher:** Erin Siegal McIntyre and Deborah Bonello, "Is Rape the Price to Pay for Chasing the American Dream?" Fusion.net, September 10, 2014.

Chapter 18

208 **a national water shortage emergency:** "El Salvador Declares Drought Emergency for First Time Ever," Reuters, April 14, 2016, reuters.com/article/us-el-salvador-drought-idUSKCN0XB2YM.

208 **Some 3.5 million people in Central America:** "Central America Drought: 2014–16," *Relief Web,* reliefweb.int/disaster/dr-2014-000132-hnd.

Chapter 19

214 **There were no** *permisos***:** Julia Preston, "Migrants Flow in South Texas, as Do Rumors," *New York Times,* June 16, 2014.

Afterword

229 **Appalling conditions in adult detention centers:** Wil S. Hylton, "The Shame of America's Family Detention Camps," *New York Times Magazine,* February 4, 2015.

229 **no longer outsource incarceration:** United States Department of Justice, "Phasing Out Our Use of Private

Prisons," *Justice Blogs,* August 18, 2016, justice.gov/opa/blog/phasing-out-our-use-private-prisons.

229 **initiating new contracts:** Madison Pauly, "The Private Prison Industry Is Licking Its Chops Over Trump's Deportation Plans," *Mother Jones,* February 21, 2017.

229 **since he was elected:** Caitlin Huston, "Gun Stocks Fall and Prison Stocks Jump after Trump Win," *MarketWatch,* November 9, 2016, marketwatch.com/story/gun-stocks-fall-and-prison-stocks-jump-after-trump-win-2016-11-09.

230 **deported over 450,000 people:** Immigration and Customs Enforcement, "FY 2015 ICE Immigration Removals," US Department of Homeland Security, ice.gov/removal-statistics/2015#wcm-survey-target-id; Office of Immigration Statistics, "DHS Immigration Enforcement: 2016," *Annual Flow Report,* US Department of Homeland Security, dhs.gov/sites/default/files/publications/DHS%20Immigration%20Enforcement%202016.pdf.

230 **9 percent of total removals:** Immigration and Customs Enforcement, "FY 2015 ICE Immigration Removals," US Department of Homeland Security, ice.gov/removal-statistics/2015#wcm-survey-target-id.

230 **more than any administration to date:** Human Rights Watch, "United States: Events of 2016," 2016, hrw.org/world-report/2017/country-chapters/united-states.

230 **prosecution for facilitating smuggling:** DHS Memo, "Implementing the President's Border Security and Immigration Enforcement Improvements Policies," February 20, 2017.

231 **as those fluent in English:** Lesli A. Maxwell, "Stemming the Tide of English-Learner Dropouts," *Education Week,* March 14, 2013, blogs.edweek.org/edweek/learning -the-language/2013/03/stemming_the_tide_of_english-l .html?cmp=ENL-EU-NEWS2.

231 **without a high school diploma:** "National Unemployment Rate Steady, but Those Without a High School Diploma Still Struggle," Employment Policy Institute, April 2010, epionline.org/release/national-unemployment -rate-steady-but-those-without-a-high-school-diploma-still -struggle/.

231 **high school diploma or equivalent:** "Educational Attainment in the United States: 2015," United States Census Bureau, March 2016, census.gov/content/dam/Census/library /publications/2016/demo/p20-578.pdf.

232 **increase national earnings by $1.2 billion:** "Saving Future, Saving Dollars: The Impact of Education on Crime Reduction and Earnings," The Alliance for Excellence in Education, September 2013, all4ed.org/wp-content/uploads /2013/09/SavingFutures.pdf.

INDEX

ABOUT THE AUTHOR

LAUREN MARKHAM is a writer based in Berkeley, California, focusing on issues related to youth, migration, the environment, and her home state of California. Her work has appeared in outlets such as *Harper's*, *The New Republic*, *Orion*, *The Guardian*, the *New York Times*, and *VQR*, where she is a contributing editor. Lauren earned her MFA in Fiction Writing from Vermont College of Fine Arts. For over a decade, she has worked in the fields of refugee resettlement and immigrant education.